Immeasurably Deeper

Immeasurably Deeper

A 40-day devotional
for a deeper life in the Spirit

Edited by
Abby Guinness

MONARCH
BOOKS

Oxford UK, and Grand Rapids, USA

Published by Monarch Books (an imprint of Lion Hudson plc)
Wilkinson House, Jordan Hill Road, Oxford OX2 8DR, England
Email: monarch@lionhudson.com www.lionhudson.com/monarch
and by Elevation (an imprint of the Memralife Group)
Memralife Group, 14 Horsted Square, Uckfield, East Sussex TN22 1QG
Tel: +44 (0)1825 746530; Fax +44 (0)1825 748899;
www.elevationmusic.com

ISBN 978 0 85721 648 9
e-ISBN 978 0 85721 649 6

First edition 2015

Acknowledgments
Unless otherwise noted Scripture quotations are taken from the Holy Bible, New International Version, copyright © 1973, 1978, 1984 International Bible Society. Used by permission of Hodder & Stoughton, a member of the Hodder Headline Group. All rights reserved. "NIV" is a trademark of International Bible Society. UK trademark number 1448790.

Scripture quotations marked ESV are from The Holy Bible, English Standard Version® (ESV®) copyright © 2001 by Crossway, a publishing ministry of Good News Publishers. All rights reserved.

Scripture quotations marked LB are taken from The Holy Bible, Living Bible Edition, copyright © Tyndale House Publishers 1971. All rights reserved.

Scripture quotations marked MSG are taken from The Message. Copyright © by Eugene H. Peterson 1993, 1994, 1995, 1996, 2000, 2001, 2002. Used by permission of NavPress Publishing Group.

Scripture quotations marked NASB are taken from the New American Standard Bible®, Copyright © 1960, 1962, 1963, 1968, 1971, 1972, 1973, 1975, 1977, 1995 by The Lockman Foundation. Used by permission.

Scripture quotations marked NET are from the NET Bible® copyright ©1996– 2006 by Biblical Studies Press, L.L.C. http://bible.org All rights reserved. Used by permission.

Contributors: Gavin Calver, Mark Greene, Abby Guinness, Michele Guinness, Katharine Hill, Krish Kandiah, Virginia Luckett, Cathy Madavan, Medea Peabody, Rob Peabody, Cris Rogers, Dot Tyler, Ruth Valerio.

With thanks to all the contributors, and to Alice O'Kane and Miranda Lever.

A catalogue record for this book is available from the British Library

Printed and bound in the United Kingdom, January 2015, LH26

Blessed are those who trust in the Lord… they shall be like a tree planted by water, sending out its roots by the stream. It shall not fear when heat comes, and its leaves shall stay green; in the year of drought it is not anxious, and it does not cease to bear fruit.

Jeremiah 17:7–8 (NRSV)

… the fruit of the Spirit is love, joy, peace, patience, kindness, goodness, faithfulness, gentleness and self-control.

Galatians 5:22–23 (TNIV)

You may want to work through these devotionals in forty days, for Lent, or any other season. If you have longer, we would recommend reading one per week over forty weeks, choosing to take more time pressing deeper into relationship with God and his life-giving Spirit. This will give you a chance to implement the suggestions, ideas, and practices suggested throughout the week and explore how they might be applied specifically to your situation. You will find it helpful to have a Bible nearby as longer passages are referenced rather than printed in full.

In engaging with God and his Spirit through this resource, we pray that you will find deep refreshment, which will, in turn, bring refreshment to others.

CONTENTS

1	Prayer	11
2	Confession	14
3	Meditation	17
4	Scripture	20
5	Posture	24
6	Breathing	28
7	Worship	32
8	Fasting	35
9	Being Available	38
10	Waiting on the Spirit	41
11	Feeding Your Soul	45
12	Silence	49
13	Sabbath	52
14	Retreat	55
15	Submission	58
16	Humility	61
17	Daring to Be Desperate	64
18	Striving	67
19	Expectancy	70
20	Drawing Closer to God	73
21	Intentionality	77
22	Sacrifice	80
23	Resurrection	83
24	Leading into Deeper	86

25	Listening (to God and Others)	90
26	Asking	93
27	Thankfulness	96
28	Celebration	99
29	Disappointment	102
30	Hope	106
31	Heaven on Earth	109
32	Grief	112
33	Anxiety and Worry	115
34	Work	118
35	Worship as Lifestyle	122
36	Simplicity	125
37	Generosity	128
38	Community Life	131
39	Unity	134
40	Trust	138
	About the Authors	141

1

PRAYER

To pray is to change. Prayer is the central avenue God uses to transform us. If we are unwilling to change, we will abandon prayer as a noticeable characteristic of our lives.

Richard Foster, *Celebration of Discipline*

SOMETHING TO READ

Here's what I want you to do. Find a quiet, secluded place so you won't be tempted to role-play before God. Just be there as simply and honestly as you can manage. The focus will shift from you to God, and you will begin to sense his grace.

The world is full of so-called prayer warriors who are prayer-ignorant. They're full of formulas and programs and advice, peddling techniques for getting what you want from God. Don't fall for that nonsense. This is your Father you are dealing with, and he knows better than you what you need. With a God like this loving you, you can pray very simply.

Matthew 6:6–9 (MSG)

SOMETHING TO THINK ABOUT

Prayer, according to one ancient definition, is "keeping company with God". I believe prayer is one of the most underdeveloped spiritual disciplines of the Christian journey. In his book on the subject, Phillip Yancey says that in prayer, "I open my soul, exposing by will what God already knows by wisdom." But prayer requires things of us that we are not always willing to give. Time. Attention. Vulnerability. Submission. Transformation. And often, we feel inadequate to pray because we are stuck in works-based righteousness that makes us a slave to approaching prayer as a vending machine or a crown jewel in a glass case. Perfection as a means and/or an end to prayer is not the answer.

What if prayer is the constant act of learning? If the disciples had prayed all their lives, but desperately needed Jesus to teach them (Luke 11:1), how much more do we need our Lord to engage with us in our intercession, showing us what and how to pray? Jesus commanded that his disciples pray, conveying a certainty that it could make a difference in a world opposed to the will of God. Even though Jesus appeared to create a formula for what prayer should look like (Matthew 6:9), we instinctively know this was a mere glimpse of the attitude in which to come before the Father.

Prayer is not the collection of the right words any more than it is the motivating factor to obtain our deepest worldly desires. In prayer, we are constantly learning the contextual heart of the Father. We come to realize that prayer is not just an inner dialogue taking place, but the Spirit of God is praying within us and communicating his will. Because of this, we may "approach God's throne of grace with confidence, so that we may receive mercy and find grace to help us in our time of need" (Hebrews 4:16, TNIV).

SOMETHING TO TRY

Over the next week, begin praying for something you care deeply about. Spend time with the Father each day on this one subject, trying different prayers. Commit to learning how to pray for this one intercessory subject. Be sure to draw near to God through each prayer, learning how he wants you to pray.

Some questions to ask God:

- *What is your will?*
- *What would please you?*
- *How can this advance your kingdom?*

SOMETHING TO PRAY

> **Our Father in heaven,**
> **Reveal who you are.**
> **Set the world right;**
> **Do what's best –**
> **as above, so below.**
> **Keep us alive with three square meals.**
> **Keep us forgiven with you and forgiving others.**
> **Keep us safe from ourselves and the Devil.**
> **You're in charge!**
> **You can do anything you want!**
> **You're ablaze in beauty!**
> **Yes. Yes. Yes.**
>
> **Matthew 6:9–13 (MSG)**

2

CONFESSION

AG

If we say that we have no sin, we deceive ourselves, and the truth is not in us. If we confess our sins, he who is faithful and just will forgive us our sins and cleanse us from all unrighteousness.

1 John 1:8–9 (NRSV)

Therefore confess your sins to one another, and pray for one another, so that you may be healed. The prayer of the righteous is powerful and effective.

James 5:16 (NRSV)

SOMETHING TO READ

Nehemiah 1:1–10

SOMETHING TO THINK ABOUT

When sharing a bedroom with my brother when we were little, if we'd been talking or causing mischief, as the bedroom door creaked open and a parent appeared, before anything could be said I would instantly, and loudly, announce (with a pointed finger to eliminate doubt), "It was him!"

I've never liked admitting guilt. But growing up with the Anglican liturgy I have always loved the helpful routine of asking for forgiveness for those things we have done purposefully or might have done unwittingly or by omission.

We need to confess our sins to God, to acknowledge to him where we have marred his image in us. To omit confession is to make ourselves God, and judge that we are capable of deciding what is right and wrong. A routine searching of the self for where we have made ourselves higher than we ought is an opportunity for the Spirit to work in us.

In some cases, we also need to confess to others.

There was a time when I was running headlong into something damaging, not only to me but to others, so I asked a friend to hold me accountable. She faithfully asked me how it was going and I convincingly lied. I couldn't bear to tell anyone how badly I'd failed, how willingly I'd given in to temptation and done what was wrong. There were mercifully no repercussions so I didn't need to tell anyone, and I didn't for several years.

The memory of it, however, would regularly pop up during the times when I was most trying to connect with God or serve in church. Finally, after it had waved itself under my nose at yet another unwelcome moment I dragged a friend into the garden and blurted it all out. I said, "I know what I did was wrong and I'm sorry. And I know God has already forgiven me. But the memory of it won't leave me alone because no one else knows." Liz listened without condemnation. She prayed for me. I didn't cry or feel anything particularly special. But the memory of that sinful incident has never bothered me again.

Confession to God was important and I did it so many times. Confession to another person, along with prayer, was what made me able to finally accept God's forgiveness deep into my subconscious, instead of just knowing it in my head. Without fireworks, the Spirit dissolved the issue so it could no longer be a blockage to my knowledge of forgiveness or to God working through me.

SOMETHING TO TRY

Use the prayer below. Take a moment to pause after the word "sins" and consider what they might have been for you in the last twenty-four hours. Leave them behind as you continue the prayer. You could consider making this a daily, weekly or monthly routine.

If there is a particular action, thought, or relationship that always jumps into your mind to remind you of your sinfulness, find someone outside of the situation to whom you can safely confess. Let them pray for you.

SOMETHING TO PRAY

> **Almighty God, our heavenly Father,**
> **we have sinned against you**
> **and against our neighbour,**
> **in thought and word and deed,**
> **through negligence, through weakness,**
> **through our own deliberate fault.**
> **We are truly sorry**
> **and repent of all our sins.**
> **For the sake of your Son Jesus Christ,**
> **who died for us,**
> **forgive us all that is past**
> **and grant that we may serve you in newness of life**
> **to the glory of your name.**
> **Amen.**

3

MEDITATION

CM

**Let the words of my mouth and the meditation of my heart
be acceptable in your sight,
O Lord, my rock and my redeemer.**

Psalm 19:14 (ESV)

SOMETHING TO READ
Psalm 19:1–14

SOMETHING TO THINK ABOUT
My life requires me to be something of an organizational ninja. Like you, my day consists of different boxes – a work box, a volunteering box, a family box, a friend box, a chores box and, with two teenage girls, I have a particularly large taxi-driving box. I wake up in the morning ready to consult my colour-coded online diary and my up-to-the-minute to-do list so that I can mentally schedule my day and get those boxes ticked.

Is it just me, or has life got exhausting?

So how in the world, in the midst of the chaos, can we think about meditation or focusing quietly upon God? Is it even possible to contemplate contemplating anything for more than a nanosecond?

Perhaps, like me, you have had to face the uncomfortable truth that we generally make time for what matters to us most. We may say that God is first and foremost in our lives but our diary might beg to differ. I may say I don't have time to pray or to meditate upon Scripture, but I also manage to talk about the latest boxed set series I have found time to digest or the latest project I have managed. And while of course we can do all things for God and with God, sometimes we need to actually rest in his presence and focus on our loving heavenly Father. Our busy souls long for it.

But where and how do we start? Psalm 19 is a great inspiration, and although the last verse is the most famous (thanks, Boney M!) it is everything preceding it that teaches us about how the psalmist, David, reflects upon God. Firstly, David soaks up the wonders of creation, taking in the grandeur and majesty of our maker. But he doesn't stop there. David then considers the truths and the commandments of God and how sweet and rewarding it is to walk in his ways. But the psalm doesn't stop there either. He then confesses his "presumptuous sins" and declares again his deep desire to be clean and blameless before his maker.

Creation. Commandments. Cleansing. David wonderfully meanders through the valleys of God's goodness and captures those thoughts in his songs, words and actions. Sometimes, I too find it helpful to sing a song to God or to write about a particular line of Scripture. Other times, as unskilled as I am, I try to draw the details of a flower or the contours of a landscape. Some days, I know that walking by the river while listening to inspiring music will focus my thoughts best, while another day I will need to just sit still so that my hectic mind can unravel enough for the Spirit to whisper above the constant mental clutter.

I wonder what works best for you? Where do you find those contemplative spaces that allow you to fix your focus upon God and be still in your soul? Perhaps you could find a way to do it more regularly. It might even be an idea to put it in the diary.

SOMETHING TO TRY

Find a quiet spot and imagine yourself taking a path through the normal forest of thoughts that fill your mind until you find a sunny, quiet clearing where you can sit still with God. If other thoughts pop up, acknowledge them and let them go back into the forest. If it helps you to focus, repeat the word "maranatha" slowly – it is an Aramaic word from the language of Jesus and it means, "Come, Lord". Now, in the stillness, think of one aspect of God or Psalm 19 and talk to him about it. You might want to draw, sing, or write about what you discover as you mentally sit in the clearing.

SOMETHING TO PRAY

Heavenly Father, you tell us in your word that when we seek you we will find you.

Thank you that as I meditate upon you, your creation, your truths, and your word, that your Spirit is at work in me.

Thank you Lord, that I can be still and dwell in your presence and know that in all of the busyness, you are God.

4

SCRIPTURE

CR

The Bible can feel like a meal that is too much for us to take in. We are overwhelmed and don't know where to start, but we need to chew more.

D. L. Moody said, "The Bible was not given to increase our knowledge; it was given to change our lives."

> *All Scripture is God-breathed and is useful for teaching, rebuking, correcting and training in righteousness...*
>
> **2 Timothy 3:16**

SOMETHING TO READ

> *Blessed is the man who does not walk in the counsel of the wicked or stand in the way of sinners or sit in the seat of mockers. But his delight is in the law of the Lord, and on his law he meditates day and night. He is like a tree planted by streams of water, which yields its fruit in season and whose leaf does not wither. Whatever he does prospers. Not so the wicked! They are like chaff that the wind blows away.*
>
> **Psalm 1:1–4**

SOMETHING TO THINK ABOUT

You can't help but notice the rise in keep-fit DVDs at Christmas and in January. Fitness suddenly appears on our radar as midnight of the new year arrives. Many of us, deep down, know we need to be fitter but don't have the energy or commitment to see through the process of getting fit.

The truth we all know is that what we eat either makes us healthy or can make us fat! Our physical well-being depends on our diet. With the right vitamins and minerals we keep our body at peak fitness but with the wrong food we become flabby and shapeless.

The same is true with our souls. If we spend our lives doing nothing but watching soaps, chat shows, and quizzes on TV we become lazy and lethargic. It's like junk food for the soul! If the things we eat can cause us real harm, the things we read or see can do the same. The things we consume can poison our souls. Pornography is an easy example, but what about raunchy novels? Daytime TV? Very right-wing or very left-wing newspapers? All that we read and see on the TV is like food, not for our bellies but for our very beings.

The psalmist writes in Psalm 1 that a person who is blessed watches who they walk with, whose council they keep, and what humour they are surrounded by. This righteous person delights in the law of the Lord and meditates on it day and night. In other words, someone who is going deeper with God and capturing the "immeasurably more" of God's kingdom in the world, is someone who is meditating on God's law.

Firstly, what's "law"? The Law is the first five books of the Bible: Genesis, Exodus, Leviticus, Numbers, and Deuteronomy. These five books make up the Hebrew Law or "Torah". The Bible as we know it didn't exist then, but the Torah was the beginning of the life of this beautiful book. So, someone who is going deeper with God is someone who is meditating on his book, his story, his revelation, his love letter… the Bible.

Secondly, what's "meditating" on Scripture? The psalmists didn't write in English but in Hebrew. The word we translate as meditate here is "yehgeh". *Yehgeh* is a muttering or growling noise made out loud, like the noise made by someone eating very loudly. If you have ever had a group of young people around, most probably boys, and you serve up pizza, as they eagerly chew on the cheese and it dribbles down their chin, that's *yehgeh.* So in other words, a blessed person chews and eats God's words.

I wonder if we pick at God's book like a bowl of nuts rather than devour it like a three-course meal? Psalm 1 invites us to not pick at God's law, but meditate, devour, chew, and metabolize it. We're not expected to leave it there but turn it into food for the poor, service for those in need, and empowering for the disempowered. Chewing on God's word is less about what we get from it and more about what we do with it. Does God's great meal of Scripture become energy for us to see the world radically changed by his good news?

SOMETHING TO TRY

We can become so overwhelmed by the Bible that we never start anywhere. Why not think about reading a small passage of the Gospels each day. Try reading a small section and slowly build up each week. It's too easy to read long sections and not "meditate" on it. Remember that reading the Bible isn't a reading challenge but readings that challenge. Try reading less but allowing yourself time to really chew upon its meaning in and for your life.

SOMETHING TO PRAY

Lord, as I read the psalms,
let me hear you singing.
As I read your words,
let me hear you speaking.
As I reflect on each page,
let me see your image.
And as I seek to put your precepts into practice,
let my heart be filled with joy.
Amen.

Gregory of Nazianzus (329–89)

5
POSTURE

AG

Whenever the unclean spirits saw him, they fell down before him and shouted, "You are the Son of God!"

Mark 3:11 (NRSV)

Then Moses and Aaron went away from the assembly to the entrance of the tent of meeting; they fell on their faces, and the glory of the Lord appeared to them.

Numbers 20:6 (NRSV)

SOMETHING TO READ

This is a short passage from the *New Bible Commentary* referring to Ephesians 3:14, "For this reason I kneel before the Father…"

> *The final part of Paul's prayer-report forms its climax. Here we see Paul prostrating himself before God, on his knees with head bowed to the ground, as one making obeisance and bringing a matter of utmost urgency to a powerful king (the more usual position for prayer was standing). Paul certainly wanted to convey the impression of God's power.*

Max Turner in *New Bible Commentary* (edited by D. A. Carson, R. T. France, A. Motyer, and G. J. Wenham)

SOMETHING TO THINK ABOUT

Have you heard the term "face-plant"? A skateboarder, a toddler, anyone, falls over head first, "planting" their face into the floor, and people laugh. Harsh. We use "falling flat on your face" as a description of humiliation and failure. However, all through the Bible, Old Testament and New, people are purposefully face-planting. Although lots of our modern Bible translations use the Latin word "prostrate", in both Hebrew and Greek it's described simply as, "falling on your face". It was not a cultural necessity to lie face down in respect or submission – it was either a choice or an instinctive response.

People fall in terror, in awe, in thanks, in adoration, worship, or pleading. Jesus falls on his face when he prays, "remove this cup from me" before continuing, "yet, not my will but yours be done" (Luke 22:42, NRSV). Most of the instances occur when someone is in direct communication with God – hearing from him or desperately seeking his intervention.

We may kneel to pray sometimes, we may feel desperate, but how often do we literally fall face down? Well, it takes up a lot of space, the floor's not too clean, it's not very dignified, and it's too much like hard work to get back up again. But there is power in posture. Experts say that body language is around 55 per cent of communication, with tone of voice next, and words the smallest factor. What if we were to physically communicate with God – to express, by acting out – where we are in the conversation and, by comparison, where he is? What if, as in Numbers 20:6, the glory of the Lord were to appear as a result?

I think of the verse in Romans where we're assured that the Spirit intercedes for God's people because we don't know what we ought to pray and don't have the words (Romans 8:26–27). Our posture can be a way of communicating with the Spirit when words aren't enough, and can be a helpful commitment to listen for longer, helping to open our ears and hearts.

SOMETHING TO TRY

Choose to lie face down on the floor, or kneel with your forehead on the ground, and wait for the presence of God. Whether you're an evening or morning person, choose the time you're least likely to fall asleep! If you're struggling with a wandering mind, slowly think of all the words you can use to describe the great God at whose feet you lie.

You could purposefully choose to do this in a particular place, somewhere that feels like holy ground to you, or a place where you want to see God working. (I have been known to do this in my workplace, on a mountain, and once in a cemetery, but I do try to choose a moment when no one is around.)

You might want to tell him why you have taken the posture in this instance – to humble yourself, to beg for mercy in a particular situation, to seek his presence or hear from him, to remind yourself of his greatness, in obedience to a calling, or as an act of thankfulness.

SOMETHING TO PRAY

> **God you are more knowing than all the world's wisdom.**
> **God you are more abundant than all the world's riches.**
> **God you are more powerful than all the world's rulers.**

I have nothing. I am nothing.
I am content in your presence.
If you are with me, I want nothing.

I am here. I am listening.
Tell me whatever you want to say.

6

BREATHING

CR

Breathe on me, breath of God,
Fill me with life anew
That I may love what Thou dost love,
And do what Thou wouldst do.

Edwin Hatch, 1878

SOMETHING TO READ

Then the Lord God formed a man from the dust
of the ground and breathed into his nostrils the
breath of life, and the man became a living being.
Genesis 2:7 (TNIV)

SOMETHING TO THINK ABOUT

On average, any person will take in around 20,000 breaths
a day. Each of these moments of taking in oxygen helps
us to pump blood around our body and get energy from
the food we eat. We might eat well but if we don't breathe
well we will not be getting the full amount of energy that
we could. The way we breathe can affect our physical and
mental well-being.

Correct breathing can help reduce stress levels, boost
the immune system, and even help combat insomnia and
depression. Many of us don't realize that we need the right

balance of carbon dioxide and oxygen to thrive. Breathing too fast (or too slow) has an impact on our biology and our health.

And many of us never give breathing a second thought.

The psalmist writes, "Be still, and know that I am God" (Psalm 46:10, TNIV). Being still, stopping and focusing on God, slows our whole being down. This slowing allows us to breathe in what is really happening around us. When we are stressed or pressured, we move quicker and respond faster, but often don't make better choices.

Be still, and know that I am God.

Being still causes us to slow down and take in all that needs taking in. In Genesis we are told that when God breathed into Adam's nostrils, Adam became a living being. The word translated here as breathe or breath is the word *ruach* and is also translated as wind or spirit. It is in God's breathing that we get given the Spirit of life. As Job says, "The Spirit of God has made me, and the breath of the Almighty gives me life" (Job 33:4, ESV). As we learn to connect with our breath and respond to God through it, not only does it help our emotional being but it also engages our spiritual being.

The same Spirit that raised Jesus from the dead is available to us too as God breathes into our nostrils his gift of life.

SOMETHING TO TRY

Spiritual Breathing

Many of us don't think about our physical breathing, in the same way we don't often think about our spiritual breathing. Spiritual breathing is the process of exhaling all our impure thoughts, pain, anger, sin, and frustration, then inhaling God's presence and Spirit.

If we aren't daily taking in God's Spirit, engaging with his presence, then life can quickly become a roller coaster we struggle to control.

Why not try engaging with your breathing? Sit in a still place and become aware of a comfortable breathing rhythm. First, focus on your exhaling. As you do, try confessing your sin, becoming aware of what you're getting rid of. Breathe out your pain, frustrations, anger, grief, and impure thoughts.

Then, focus on your inhaling. Each breath you take in, invite the Holy Spirit to take over you afresh. Ask for his renewing, restoring, and the empowering of his presence.

Breath prayer

Breath prayer is an ancient Christian practice dating back to the sixth century. This early practice involved breathing out in a rhythm while repeating the phrase, "Lord Jesus Christ, Son of God, have mercy on me a sinner." Followers of Jesus would do this for five to ten minutes as they focused on the phrase and allowed the Spirit to be breathed in. You don't need to use this phrase – you could try it with something more personal to you. Suggestions might be, "Less of me and more or you", "Holy one heal me", or, "Father, let me feel your presence".

SOMETHING TO PRAY

Breathe in me, O Holy Spirit, that my thoughts may all be holy.
Act in me, O Holy Spirit, that my work, too, may be holy.
Draw my heart, O Holy Spirit, that I love but what is holy.

Strengthen me, O Holy Spirit, to defend all that is holy.
Guard me, then, O Holy Spirit, that I always may be holy.
Amen.

St Augustine

7

WORSHIP

CM

Perfect submission, all is at rest!
I in my Saviour am happy and blest,
Watching and waiting, looking above,
Filled with His goodness, lost in His love.

Fanny Crosby, "Blessed Assurance", 1873

SOMETHING TO READ

1 Chronicles 16:23–34

SOMETHING TO THINK ABOUT

I recently finished reading the autobiography of Fanny Crosby who wrote over 8,000 hymns including, "To God be the Glory" and "Blessed Assurance". She was an inspiring woman who lived her life surrendered to God and his purposes, never complaining about being blind from soon after birth due to a doctor's mistake. In fact, Fanny Crosby once said that if she was given the opportunity to have her sight back she would turn it down as she feared that she would have been distracted by so many other things instead of focusing on God. I have to say, speaking as a woman married to a man who lost his sight in his twenties, I find that kind of statement awe-inspiring. It makes me wonder what kind of sacrifice I would be willing to make to ensure that I retain a 20/20 vision of God with the many distractions and attractions fighting for my attention.

Fanny Crosby's faith is a reminder that the problem is not that we forget to worship, it is that we fix our eyes on other things which become the object of our worship and attention. In our twenty-first-century culture, that other thing is often ourselves.

It is worth recalling the Greek myth where Narcissus, an incredibly handsome and proud man, was led by Nemesis to a pool, where he became fixated by his own reflection, until he could not move and drowned. I feel fairly sure that if Narcissus was not a myth and was with us today he would undoubtedly have a smart phone with a camera and a few million social media followers. The selfie, it seems, has become the new pool of reflection in which people endlessly admire themselves from a favourably filtered perspective. Could it be that a generation are now more interested in self-adoration or self-advertisement than honest self-appraisal? But we are woefully short-sighted when we replace God with ourselves, our own desires, and our own ambitions.

Perhaps we need a sight check. John 3:30 gives us one as we read that he (God) must increase and we must decrease.

It is not that self-worth is unimportant; it is more accurately that in "worship" we choose to give worth to God above everything else. And in seeing him more clearly, we see ourselves reflected in his image, made in his likeness, and loved as children of the "King of kings".

Worshipping God is a fundamental part of our spiritual life. God is always worth our worship, and giving him the praise he deserves should never be dictated by our changing moods, our circumstances, or whether we like the song choices on a Sunday. While these things can understandably affect us we must remember, as did Fanny Crosby, that nothing and no person will ever be as beautiful, captivating, full of justice and truth, faithful, or compassionate as God. He is an endless pool of living water and our lives should reflect more of his beauty than our own. If other things are restricting our spiritual vision or distracting our attention, then it is time to gaze on his majesty once again.

SOMETHING TO TRY

How could you punctuate your day by worshipping God? Try putting on worship music and taking five minutes to thank and praise God for all he is and all he has done. Or maybe there is an inspiring photo or verse that lifts your eyes to him. Take time today to actively surrender your distractions to God, so that your spiritual vision is not impaired.

SOMETHING TO PRAY

> This is my story, this is my song.
> Praising my Saviour, all the day long!
> **Fanny Crosby, "Blessed Assurance"**

> Lord God, help me to remove the obstacles in my vision that shield my view of you. I pray that I would worship you above my own needs and in all circumstances. You alone deserve the highest praise.

8

FASTING

KK

Is not this the kind of fasting I have chosen: to loose the chains of injustice and untie the cords of the yoke, to set the oppressed free and break every yoke? Is it not to share your food with the hungry and to provide the poor wanderer with shelter – when you see the naked, to clothe them, and not to turn away from your own flesh and blood? Then your light will break forth like the dawn, and your healing will quickly appear; then your righteousness will go before you, and the glory of the Lord will be your rear guard.

Isaiah 58:6–9 (TNIV)

SOMETHING TO READ

Isaiah 58:1–14

SOMETHING TO THINK ABOUT

The Great British Bake Off, Master Chef, Hell's Kitchen. Watching TV makes me hungry. Not to mention all the advertisements encouraging me to buy a chocolate bar to make me feel happy, a bottle of beer so that I would have more interesting friends, or a biological yoghurt or breakfast cereal to help me get healthy. Even if there were no external influences on me encouraging me to eat I have a very strong personal motivator – an angry stomach that has a homing device that drags me towards the fridge at odd times of the day. Often it feels like my relationship with food is about suppressing my appetite yet food is more than a temptation. It is a gift.

Before anything was wrong with the world there was food. The first food was pleasing to the eye and the tongue. Food is a gift from our generous God: our food is a daily provision from our faithful God and the variety of the food we enjoy is a blessing from our creative God. When we eat with gratitude we honour the faithful, creative provision of our God.

Yet the Bible says that we can honour God by choosing to say no to our legitimate desire for food in order to increase our desire for God. The Bible says we can say no to our need for food in order to demonstrate our dependence on God. Throughout Scripture at times of national emergency, when God's people sought wisdom, deliverance, or wanted to express regret and remorse they called a fast. Fasting can help develop our hunger for God. By going without food we can give God more of our time and our attention, so it is a very powerful way we can express our worship to him.

At one level to say, "No" to something so essential to life might seem to be part of the highest worship we could offer to God. For us to deliberately choose to experience some pain and discomfort in order to prioritize God in our lives is a very bold kind of adoration.

But God is clear in the passage above that fasting is not valuable in itself. Fasting could be an attempt to manipulate God. We might think that fasting is like a turbo boost for our prayers – if I fast when I pray it adds more power to my requests of God. Or we might think that fasting is a way of gaining a reputation of spirituality in the eyes of our believing friends. But even if you fast with a pure motive – to honour God – even then God says to us if our worship of him is simply a decision to go without food while we ignore those who are hungry because of their poverty (rather than their acts of piety) our fasting is worthless. God is honoured when we attend to the needs of those around us. Our spirituality, no matter how sacrificial, cannot mean closing our eyes to the needs of the oppressed, marginalized, and hungry.

SOMETHING TO TRY

Invite someone you know who is going through a hard time to share some food with you. As you buy or prepare the food for your guest reflect on God's provision in your life. The next day, if your health allows it, deliberately skip a meal in order to spend time with God. As you sense your physical hunger rising, ask that God would increase your hunger for him.

SOMETHING TO PRAY

> Our Father in heaven,
> hallowed be your name,
> your kingdom come,
> your will be done,
> on earth as it is in heaven.
> Give us today our daily bread...

9

BEING AVAILABLE

CM

My sheep listen to my voice; I know them, and they follow me.

John 10:27

SOMETHING TO READ

Mark 1:16–20

SOMETHING TO THINK ABOUT

About two years ago I decided that enough was enough. I had spent years with an old radio, waggling the aerial wildly in different directions in the hope that I might pick up the voice of a human in the audio blizzard. I had tried placing the radio upon various shelves and tweaking the dial again and again, vainly believing that I would miraculously find a signal. But it never worked. And so finally we took the plunge and bought a digital radio. What a revelation! Not only were the mainstream channels as clear as a bell but I realized that there are dozens of other, previously unheard of, stations that were now available too. All I had to do was work out which one I wanted to listen to.

I have a hunch that my spiritual and emotional antennae could also sometimes do with an upgrade. I find myself lost in a blizzard of stress or self-sufficiency, becoming barricaded and unwittingly tuning out from those around me, and even sometimes from God.

But at other times I feel more like my digital radio: able to be accessed by everybody all of the time, wherever I am. But can I be constantly on air and open for business to whomever and whenever? In my desire to be available, do I become incapable of saying no or knowing whom to listen to?

When I look at Jesus, I see a man who felt able to connect but also to withdraw as he was on his Father's business, committed to doing only what his Father asked him to do (John 6:38). We are called to clearly imitate our good shepherd and to then be thoroughly present and available to those he asks us to serve. We can never be there for everybody, but we really can be there for somebody. We can't say yes to every opportunity but we should passionately commit to serving where God asks us. We can't really know the hundreds of people we may follow on Twitter, but the question is whether we are tuned in and listening when Jesus asks us to follow him.

As we actively open our spiritual ears to God's whispers, and discern where he is, and is not, guiding us, we will have enough time, energy, and wisdom to be available to those God has asked us to serve. This matters, as one of the greatest gifts we can give to others is our undivided time and attention. When we smile and talk with a frazzled supermarket assistant or read a child their favourite book for the 300th time, we must not underestimate the impact of our actions. Being available makes a difference. We have all had those conversations with somebody in the same room who is remote or difficult to reach, or waited patiently for a colleague who was more interested in their phone than in us. That kind of "interference" destroys the potential in our relationships. Today, God is asking us again to be fully available to him so that we can hear his voice and be genuinely available to others.

SOMETHING TO TRY

Wherever you are today, make a vow to be available to God. Listen to his whispers and be aware of those who are in your presence. Whether it is by email, in a café, across a desk or the dinner table, consciously tune in to the spoken and unspoken needs of those whom God has placed in your way. Bless them and be available to them to do all that God asks of you.

SOMETHING TO PRAY

Lord Jesus, thank you that you have called me to do as you have done.

I confess I don't always hear you as clearly as I should, and I admit the noise of my life gets in the way of my hearing your Spirit speak.

Lord, once again I declare that I am available to you and to others – to listen, to love, and to serve, as you call me to do.

Speak; your servant is listening.

10

WAITING ON THE SPIRIT

CR

To us waiting is wasting. To God, waiting is working.

Louie Giglio

The Lord is good to those who wait for him, to the soul who seeks him.

Lamentations 3:25 (esv)

Wait for the Lord; be strong, and let your heart take courage; wait for the Lord!

Psalm 27:14 (esv)

SOMETHING TO READ

Acts 1:4–9

SOMETHING TO THINK ABOUT

Maseno is a radically poor region of Kenya found on the equator. It has the potential to be a wealthy region but because of poor farming and the spread of HIV it struggles to thrive. As part of a ministry for educating farmers we were there visiting households to understand the needs and if a farming school would be a benefit to them.

On a hot afternoon we arrived at a small *shamba* (farm) where two women were arguing. Tugging a small chicken between them, there was a lot of shouting that we didn't understand. It turned out that the chicken had been given to the family and the two women were mother and daughter. The daughter wanted to kill and cook the chicken while the mother wanted to feed it and wait for eggs.

The question at hand was a cooked chicken today or an egg tomorrow?

Sometimes we have difficult decisions to make. Do we choose an immediate effect or a delayed effect giving a greater outcome? I hate waiting; it grates against everything in me in this fast-paced culture where we demand the immediate.

Jesus turned to his disciples on the day he departed and told them to go and wait. How frustrating! What time-wasting! What was the point? Couldn't they just get on with the action, telling people the good news and saving lives?

Jesus sent his friends off to wait, not because it would take weeks to happen but because, I believe, there is a direct link to waiting on the Spirit and receiving the Spirit. Waiting is active not passive. Jesus shows us that going off and waiting isn't the absence of action, it is in fact the action of being present, persevering, and orienting your heart towards Jesus. Waiting is doing the most important thing – investing in a relationship and showing yourself as well as God that you need more of him. Waiting tells us we aren't in charge; we can't demand God to work to our timetable.

In the Old Testament the word most often translated as "to wait" is that of *qavah*. *Qavah* is an active word that can be understood as the process "binding together" – like twisting strands of twine to make a rope. It can also be understood as to hope, expect, or look eagerly. Waiting isn't an inactive time of twiddling of thumbs, but the proactive time of twisting ourselves together with the Divine. We take time to allow God to wrap around us and us to wrap around God.

I hate waiting, but if waiting means being able to be intertwined with God, I'll wait for as long as forever to see it happen.

SOMETHING TO TRY

Waiting and hoping are two things closely intertwined. This is why the Hebrew word *qavah* is sometimes translated "hope". The ability to wait on the Lord stems from being confident and focused on who God is and on what God is doing.

Try clearing a space in your day when the home is quietest. Find a comfortable chair. As you sit, close your eyes and hold your hands out in front of you. With hope, invite God to draw close to you. Allow time to become aware of his presence.

Sometimes I have done this and felt God's presence within moments; at other times it has felt like he never showed up. I've come to realize that God's presence is always with us; it might just be me who is absent. When waiting, try to become aware of your thoughts. Don't allow them to be drawn on to your list of jobs to be done, but focus on focusing on him.

- Wait quietly.
  I wait quietly before God, for my hope is in him. Psalm 62:5 (NLT)
- Wait patiently.
  Be still in the presence of the Lord, and wait patiently for him to act. Psalm 37:7 (NLT)
- Wait expectantly.
  I wait expectantly, trusting God to help, for he has promised. Psalm 105:5 (LB)

Try doing this as often as you can. You might notice that each time waiting on God becomes easier and more empowering. Don't give up! Don't stop believing! Stay full of hope and expectation. God's power and presence is limitless, and will come like the day of Pentecost.

SOMETHING TO PRAY

> Lord, I wait on you and wait for your presence to come and restore, rebuild, and empower me for all you have called me to. Lord, I wait...

11
FEEDING YOUR SOUL

MP

**This is what the Lord says, "Stand at the crossroads and look;
ask for the ancient paths, ask where the good way is, and
walk in it; and you will find rest for your souls."**

Jeremiah 6:16

**Take my yoke upon you and learn from me, for I am gentle
and humble in heart, and you will find rest for your souls.**

Matthew 11:29 (TNIV)

SOMETHING TO READ
Psalm 63

SOMETHING TO THINK ABOUT
The soul is a complex topic with varying definitions by
philosophers from different centuries. Most would agree that
the soul is the deepest, intangible part of us. What does
the Bible tell us about the soul? When the psalmist says his
soul is "among lions" (57:4), he means *he* is there among
the lions. The writer of Hebrews describes the "saving of the
soul" (10:39) as the saving of the person. In the Bible, "soul"
indicates that with the soul comes the entirety of the person.
Dallas Willard says the "soul is that aspect of your whole
being that *correlates*, *integrates*, and *enlivens* everything

going on in the various dimensions of the self" (*Renovation of the Heart*). The soul is intimately connected to every part of our holistic selves. If that is true, then what goes into each dimension of us is congruently linked to every other part of our self.

When thinking about the word "feeding" we automatically attribute it to the act of consumption. What are you consuming? What is going in? If we can agree that we are holistic beings in which every realm of our being is connected, then what we feed ourselves is of extreme importance. Therefore, sometimes our headaches could be attributed to external stress and sometimes our stress can be attributed to a lack of prayer. Our emotional, physical, psychological, and spiritual lives cannot take a break from each other. They are intrinsically connected. Whatever you are putting into one, ultimately the others will receive. Our soul is like an internal stream of flowing water that gives nourishment, direction, and strength to all other internal elements. If our soul is intentionally rooted in the richness of God, then everything else within us is refreshed and directed by that stream.

Jesus says in Matthew 16:26, "For what will it profit a man if he gains the whole world and forfeits his soul? Or what will a man give in exchange for his soul?" (NASB). Jesus explains that if your life is not under the direction of your internal stream, then it will be ruled by the externality of superficiality. After all, the rich young man who tore down his barns to build bigger ones for his abundant produce and overly delighted in them, forfeited his soul in exchange for temporary, external, worldly pleasure (Luke 12:16–21). The prodigal son realized his licentious lifestyle did not feed his soul, and abandoned his worldly practices in favour of the one he knew would truly satisfy him (Luke 15:11–32).

How are you feeding your soul? Are you feeding it with worldly, temporary pleasures like the rich young man and the prodigal? Or are you giving the Father the time he desires from you, that you so desperately need?

SOMETHING TO TRY

Make time to contemplate and write down what your soul is consuming.

Some questions to ask yourself:

- *What are my priorities?*
- *How do I spend my time?*
- *What do I spend my money on?*
- *What am I watching or listening to?*
- *How do these things affect my inner being?*
- *How much room do I make for God? For prayer?*
- *Is my internal stream directing me or are the external superficialities of my life doing it?*
- *What steps do I need to take, if any, to create space for God to be the source of my internal stream?*

SOMETHING TO PRAY

Lord God,
All things come from you and nothing from me.
I confess my inability to feed my soul properly
and express that you are the only source that
can truly satisfy.

Jesus, You are the Bread of Life.
Jesus, You are Living Water.
Jesus, You are the True Sabbath.

Forgive me for the ways in which I have consumed toxic waste, and allowed it to penetrate my entire being. I claim your cleansing power over my soul and ask you to become my internal stream of love and guidance.

12

SILENCE

There sometimes springs an interior peace and quietude which is full of happiness, for the soul is in such a state that it thinks there is nothing that it lacks. Even speaking – by which I mean vocal prayer and meditation – wearies it: it would like to do nothing but love.

St Teresa of Avila (1515–82)

SOMETHING TO READ
Song of Songs 2:1–13

SOMETHING TO THINK ABOUT
Being an extrovert and an external processor, silence – for me – is difficult because I struggle to know what I'm thinking. Being busy means making time for silence, just silence, often seems impossible. But somehow, by the grace of God, I was able to go on my first week-long silent retreat in 2010. I had buried my mother the week before I went.

I was to see my guide – a lovely, godly, kind woman – for just half an hour each day. The first evening before the silence, I blurted out to her in a big rush about my mum, the cancer, the suffering, my spiritual chaos, my Christian journey. I spoke almost without taking breath. She said calmly and kindly, "Perhaps we are going to need forty minutes a day," and "Tomorrow, why don't you go into the garden and ask God who he wants to be for you now…"

The silence was painful because the many years of never looking inside opened up in a way I never believed possible. For five days and five nights, my mind and heart raced; raced over a thousand things a second. It was like an unravelling. Memories, emotions, ideas, dreams, hopes, disappointments, and grief welled up, spilled over, and engulfed me. My silence was loud – so loud I struggled to sleep. Awake or asleep, the noise was still there.

But then came the miracle.

Suddenly, but almost imperceptibly, the noise stopped. It was like I had been set adrift in space – a massive, unending, eternal space that somehow was inside and yet completely outside and all around. And that vast eternal space was God. There is no other way to describe it. The silence had broken through the trappings of my surface thoughts, feelings, and experiences, however hard, and had, ever so gently, ushered me into the presence of our great and glorious triune God. In that place I felt so in awe I hardly felt I could breathe for fear of disturbing the silence. I rested – rested in a way I had never rested before. I rested in my soul.

That week, and silences since, have taught me so much about God and what it means to be *in Christ*. It has given me access to a place of deep rest and immense joy that somehow travels with me. Remembering the silence is like that deep well of living water, the Holy Spirit that rises up to refresh and revive. These blissful encounters will remain with me throughout my life. They will bring me comfort when I die because I know, that having spoken no words, I am known by God in a way I never imagined possible. I praise God for his mercy and grace and the gift of silence.

SOMETHING TO TRY

Just try it! There is no shortcut to silence. It's simple: it just involves silence and God. You have everything you need. What's stopping you? Carve out time in your diary today for an extended period of silence. Organize childcare, arrange time off work, book yourself into a retreat house, switch off your phone, and prepare to meet God.

SOMETHING TO PRAY

> **Lord, God of the still small voice and the immense silence, I come.**

13

SABBATH

MGu

Six days a week we wrestle with the world, wringing profit from the earth; on the Sabbath we especially care for the seed of eternity planted in the soul. The world has our hands, but our soul belongs to Someone Else.

Rabbi Abraham Joshua Heschel, *The Sabbath*

SOMETHING TO READ

> *If you walk with me on the Sabbath and don't use it for personal reasons,*
> *If you welcome it with joy, and treat it as a special celebration,*
> *If you honour it by refusing "business as usual", making money and running here and there – then you'll be free to enjoy your God.*
> *And I'll make you ride high and soar above all the stresses of the other six days.*
> *I'll make you feast on your inheritance as my children.*

Isaiah 58:13–14 (adapted from The Message)

SOMETHING TO THINK ABOUT

Say the word "sabbath" and it usually conjures up outdated lists of hairshirt, boring don'ts. But freeing Sundays of all fun is sabbatarianism, and the opposite of God's original intention. "The sabbath", which Jesus himself modelled, "was made for man," he said (Mark 2:27). It was to be enjoyed, not abandoned.

I hadn't appreciated what a gift it was until my husband and I took a three-month sabbatical in France, where we were "trying out" retirement. Peter insisted we make Sunday a sabbath even before we managed to locate a church. And how I resented it. Isn't every day a sabbath on your sabbatical? Typical male, I thought, copping-out of doing the vital DIY. Long, lazy Sundays? He was becoming too French!

That first Sunday turned out to be a glorious day and as we biked through the peaceful countryside, I unwound. In the Hebraic tradition there should be one day a week with no buying or selling, when our employer doesn't own us, and we don't own our employees. No more hierarchy or injustice. Even the land is left to rest. It's meant to be a taste of heaven, of our eternal rest. And that was exactly how it felt. By night-time I was totally chilled, especially after a time of worship and a glass of Pineau de Charentes in front of the fire. I wished every day was Sunday.

In Exodus 19:5 God says to his people at Sinai, "Will you take me as your God?" and they respond, "We will." The ten "instructions for living" are the marriage contract, and the wedding ring, the special seal of their covenant love, is sabbath. When we did The Marriage Course in our church, every Sunday I'd see couples nudge each other, "Have you had your married time this week?" Maybe God whispers to us, "Are we getting any married time this week? Is one day in seven too much to ask?"

Christians, too, are driven by our consumer society whose goals are to accomplish, perform, and possess. We work to get and want more. Workaholism destroys both us and our relationships; robs us of joy and faith. But we don't have to be slaves to achievement, to busyness, to the instant of the smart phone or Twitter, to "the now". Sabbath, believes theologian Walter Brueggeman, is an act of resistance to our culture. It puts God back at the centre of our lives. Human freedom is expressed as much in the ability to stop work as in the ability to work. Sabbath is a chance to check out who is master of our lives – God or the idols we create. If we can't get off the merry-go-round one day in seven, we are seriously and dangerously out of spiritual kilter.

SOMETHING TO TRY

"The Sabbath is one of those phenomena – incomprehensible from the outside – that you have to live in order to understand… [a] still point in the turning world," says Rabbi Jonathan Sacks. How will you make one day a week a "still point in a turning world" for you, or for your family and friends? Jot down the things you find restorative and recreative. How will you integrate them with worship and fellowship?

SOMETHING TO PRAY

> Thank you, Lord, for giving us the gift of rest and recreation to restore us to wholeness. Help us to use it wisely to model a more fulfilling, joyous, and simpler life that will restore wholeness to the world in which we live.

14

RETREAT

GC

You're my place of quiet retreat; I wait for your Word to renew me.

Psalm 119:114 (MSG)

SOMETHING TO READ

Ecclesiastes 3:1–8. *A time for everything* – that includes retreating!

SOMETHING TO THINK ABOUT

Ever since I began in ministry I've always valued spending time with the minister that I trained under fifteen years ago. On one such occasion I travelled down to see him and we settled down for a nice coffee in a trendy café. However, the mood quickly changed when the mild-mannered man I knew well became incredibly assertive. He started tackling my personal relationship with Jesus head on. The questions began flowing: "How often are you silent before God?" "Do you ever let him lead the conversation?" "When did you last spend time with Jesus without an agenda?" "How often do you take time out and retreat with the Lord?"

I was somewhat taken aback but then he crystalized the challenge in the form of a strong analogy. "In your marriage would you get away with spending as little time with your wife as you do in your relationship with Jesus?" I was silent so he continued, "This isn't a guilt trip but simply a challenge. Relationships don't survive on tiny snippets of time; they need quality time. It's no different with God. You need to invest more time in your relationship with Jesus."

Hard though it was to hear, he was right. I was not investing enough time in my personal walk with Jesus. I'm often so busy that I don't make the time. We live in interesting days. As the Dalai Lama says, we have "more conveniences, but less time". As a result we need to intentionally make time and space to be with Jesus otherwise it won't happen. The quiet time is great and arrow prayers are brilliant but, like any relationship, quality time is needed.

As a result of that meeting things have changed. I have found myself having to take time away from others and be alone with Jesus. For me this has involved taking up running long distances. I struggle to be still and not fall asleep but when on a run of ten miles or so I find that my body looks after itself and I'm able to retreat from normal life and simply hang out with Jesus. For others they find it really helpful to block out a day and simply "kick leaves with Jesus". Without aim or agenda simply spending a day with Jesus is so good for our spiritual health. Others go on silent retreats or to a retreat centre for a break.

In essence, retreat is primarily an attitude and not a place or thing. It's choosing to step away from the noise of normality in order to engage with the Almighty. Retreating is an attitude that feels so countercultural in our fast-paced world, but is vital for our spiritual health as Christians. Whatever works best for you, please do something. Your relationship with Jesus is worth the most valuable thing you have available to give: your time.

SOMETHING TO TRY

Be brave enough to look at a week or month of your life and write down how much quality time you spent with Jesus. Compare this to how much time you spent on other things that shouldn't matter as much. Off the back of the results make some decisions about how much time you would like to be spending with the Lord and make the changes that are needed. Tell a friend and ask them to hold you to account on how you are spending your time.

If the above is too much, simply block out one whole day ASAP. Don't put anything else in that day and spend it with Jesus. At first it will be really challenging but by the end of the day I guarantee you will not regret choosing to retreat from the busyness of everyday life to spend quality time with him. Try to make this a regular habit where possible.

SOMETHING TO PRAY

Lord, I'm sorry for when I don't spend the time with you that I'd like. Help me to prioritize my time differently and I pray that as I spend time with you, you might be merciful enough to meet me in a powerful and significant way. Amen.

15
SUBMISSION

CM

For those who exalt themselves will be humbled, and those who humble themselves will be exalted.

Matthew 23:12

SOMETHING TO READ

Romans 12:3–21

SOMETHING TO THINK ABOUT

I once worked part-time invigilating exams in a naval college. This meant that I spent hours pacing up and down while men (and the occasional woman) sat in smart naval uniforms taking exams that would qualify them for another level of leadership on their vessel. Ordinarily, these highly trained officers would have been responsible for a large crew on board their ship, keeping everybody and their cargo safe and travelling in the right direction during their months at sea. But for those three hours, sitting at their desks, they were under my control. (Cue sinister laugh.) If they wanted to go to the toilet, they had to ask me. If they wanted more paper, they had to raise their hand.

Although those officers were required to submit to me, they also had to choose to do so. They didn't ask for paper begrudgingly or display an attitude about not being in control. They knew that there were times when they had to take the lead, and times when others would hold the reins, and they willingly allowed that to happen.

In a culture that screams that it is all about me because I am worth it, and where power, wealth, and status are freely idolized, the concept of submission is a powerfully prophetic statement. We Christians have the potential to model something potent in the way we deal with people. We can choose to not always be right (my husband will be thrilled to hear it). We can decide that others have an opinion worth hearing and that maybe we don't always hold all of the facts. We can honour our leaders and bless them and in turn diligently and lovingly lead and serve others when we are asked to step up to the plate. Submission should never be an issue of hierarchy or power versus lack or power; it should be about, as the apostle Paul puts it, preferring or honouring one another above ourselves (Romans 12:10).

As you and I become increasingly secure in who we are in Christ, we are able to relinquish our need to control others and trust them as we trust God. Whether we are parents, married people, church members or leaders, colleagues or friends, our role is to enable people to flourish. This means having to let go – which any parent of teenagers will tell you, is the hardest part of loving anybody. But power and control are fragile commodities built out of fear or obedience, whereas love is a strong bond offering freedom and security that will continue to flex and extend.

As always, Jesus is our example – he had authority and influence, he even knew that he was God, but he willingly submitted himself to the will of the Father – even to death on a cross. He shows us that it is strength that chooses a posture of submission but weakness that instead settles for position, pride, or power. Restrained power is always the most impressive power of all.

Today, as you and I submit to God once again, we will loosen the grip of control in our hearts and make room for the power of the Spirit to strengthen us to serve and love others – as Jesus would.

SOMETHING TO TRY

If you are able, kneel in a posture of voluntary submission before our holy and loving God. Read Philippians 2:1–11 and spend some time imagining the journey of Jesus, from heaven to earth, to the cross, to the right hand of the Father. Present yourself to him again as one who would serve him and others in confident and powerful submission.

SOMETHING TO PRAY

> **Lord God, I am sorry that I so often make myself lord of my life and that I, in my weakness, try to manipulate or control others. I submit myself to you again and ask that you would be Lord of all. Help me to serve you and to serve others today, as Jesus would. Amen.**

16

HUMILITY

RP

True humility is not thinking less of yourself; it is thinking of yourself less.

C. S. Lewis, *Mere Christianity*

SOMETHING TO READ

Philippians 2:1–11

SOMETHING TO THINK ABOUT

Our world values power and progress. Do this; achieve that; conquer so-and-so; do what it takes; the ends justify the means; work to your advantage; capitalize; push; and overcome. Society tells us that to become greater, we must build. We must work, toil, struggle, and claw our way to the top in order to really be something of great worth and respect. We should be proud of what we have accomplished, we should celebrate our achievements, we are self-made people deserving of adulation and praise. And it is no mystery where these attributes and values come from – our society comes by them naturally. For they are merely outward expressions of the natural fallen human nature, or sinful nature, that we are all inevitably born into.

Freedom is seen as something that you must obtain in order to be happy in today's world. But the irony of pursuing freedom in all areas of our lives is that we can end up becoming a slave to the very pursuit of it. The very thing that our society values (freedom) can itself become the slave master. If we can just be free to pursue the things mentioned in the paragraph above, then we can finally be satisfied and happy. This is the mantra of our world today.

On the other hand, "Humility, as we all know, is one of those virtues that is never gained by seeking it," states Richard Foster in his book *Celebration of Discipline*. The more we pursue humility, the more distant it becomes for us. Jesus gives us the alternative to living in this cycle of power, pride, and egotism, and it is a life of sacrifice and humility. A life of laying our ambition aside and choosing to love and serve. And the most amazing part about it all is that when the Spirit leads us into this life, we find true freedom. A life of humility is a life of joy.

In today's passage we see the ultimate expression of humility on display: the God who made the world humbles himself to become the lowest in the world. Setting aside all of the privileges of God-ness, Jesus took on the status of a slave. He emptied himself in a manger and on the cross when what he deserved was cosmic adulation and praise. In doing so, he set the example and the ability for his followers to live this out today. Paul writes in his letter to the Philippians that followers of Jesus should, "in humility consider others better than yourselves" and "look not only to your own interests, but also to the interests of others" (2:3, 4). Counter to the thinking of this world, this is where we find true satisfaction, joy, liberation, and freedom. By taking on the humility of Jesus we discover and can live in the freedom he died to give us.

SOMETHING TO TRY

In England, in the eighteenth century, William Law wrote a book entitled *A Serious Call to a Devout and Holy Life*, in which he urges the necessity of pursuing a life of humility connected to a life of service. He states that if we want humility we must,

> condescend to all the weaknesses and infirmities
> of your fellow-creatures, cover their frailties,
> love their excellencies, encourage their virtues,
> relieve their wants, rejoice in their prosperities,
> compassionate their distress, receive their
> friendship, overlook their unkindness, forgive their
> malice, be a servant of servants, and condescend
> to do the lowest offices to the lowest of mankind.

Law urges us to seek the discipline of service as the counter-attack to self-interest, which will result in the rise of grace and humility in our lives.

This week, identify someone that you want to serve by putting his or her interests above yours. What help do they need? How can you empathize with them and share their burdens? What is something practical you can do to serve them today? As you serve and think about them (and not you), by God's grace, the Spirit will be inching you one step closer towards a life of humility.

SOMETHING TO PRAY

Lord, please give me the grace to live out your gospel and think of myself less. Will you open my eyes and direct me to who I can put ahead of myself today?

17

DARING TO BE DESPERATE

CR

...it's the lack of a sense of desperation for God that is so deadly.

Jon Bloom, author of *Not by Sight*

Listen to my cry, for I am in desperate need; rescue me from those who pursue me, for they are too strong for me.

Psalm 142:6

SOMETHING TO READ

Psalm 142

SOMETHING TO THINK ABOUT

It was a depressing moment. It felt like everything was falling apart and that nothing was solid around me. I had made some decisions that weren't healthy and a significant relationship I was in was coming to an end. The weeks leading up to me crying out to God for one of the first times in my life included my being arrested for trespassing and then being found by a relative in an "awkward position". I had been well and truly busted and no matter how hard I tried to ignore it they had caught me doing something of which they (and, deep down, I) didn't approve. All of this led me to a place where something needed to change. I was desperate. The moment came for me to put God to the test and I cried out to him. In this place of raw desperation and depression, God came and met with me. Not with a flash of light and a loud voice but with a still, small voice that spoke significance, grace, and joy in to my life. My desperation, my feeling like I was drowning, brought me to a place of bursting out an invitation to God.

Since then I've reflected a lot on this sense of desperation. Life became better and things started to fall into place, and as they did so I became less desperate. The more things chugged along the more I put God to the sideline.

Anyone can be desperate when they are drowning like I was, with everything life throws at us piling over our heads. I've realized I have to ask myself the questions, "Can I be desperate when life isn't painful or heavy going? Can I be as desperate for God in the good times as when I am sinking?"

The word *desperate* comes from the Latin word meaning "despair". Despair is a reckless sense of being driven to take any risk. I want to have this desperate and reckless faith in God's presence and provision when life is good and bad. I don't want to be an unfair-weather follower, but rather someone who is longing for God in all seasons.

Desperate prayer in all seasons can result in a deeper knowledge of God. It inspires worship and dependence on him. This is often what happened to King David. He certainly understood it when he wrote Psalm 34:1: "I will bless the Lord at *all* times; his praise shall continually be in my mouth" (ESV). God invites us in to be desperate for him at all times, good or bad.

SOMETHING TO TRY

Read this passage – Hebrews 12:1–3:

> *Therefore, since we are surrounded by such*
> *a great cloud of witnesses, let us throw off*

everything that hinders and the sin that so easily entangles, and let us run with perseverance the race marked out for us. Let us fix our eyes on Jesus, the author and perfecter of our faith, who for the joy set before him endured the cross, scorning its shame, and sat down at the right hand of the throne of God. Consider him who endured such opposition from sinful men, so that you will not grow weary and lose heart.

Ask yourself one or all of these questions:

- *How desperate am I for Jesus to help me run the race of faith?*
- *At times when the race is easy, am I still desperate to cry out to God for his presence?*
- *Does my desperation become my motivation to reach out to Jesus?*
- *How desperate am I to experience more of God in my life?*

SOMETHING TO PRAY

Father, I dare to be desperate.
There are times when life is easy and I forget you.
I don't want to forget.
I want to become desperate for your life in me in the good times and the bad.
Father, give me a reckless faith that gives you everything so that I only depend upon you.
Help me put down the things I cling to and become someone who trusts only in you.
Help me cease to be self-sufficient and focused on fixing things myself.
Amen.

18

STRIVING

CM

It is a mistake to think that the practice of my art has become easy to me. I assure you, dear friend, no one has given so much care to the study of composition as I.

Wolfgang Amadeus Mozart

SOMETHING TO READ

> *Have nothing to do with godless myths and old wives' tales; rather, train yourself to be godly. For physical training is of some value, but godliness has value for all things, holding promise for both the present life and the life to come. This is a trustworthy saying that deserves full acceptance. That is why we labour and strive, because we have put our hope in the living God, who is the Saviour of all people, and especially of those who believe.*

1 Timothy 4:7–10

SOMETHING TO THINK ABOUT

Many of us spend a good portion of our time and energy aiming high and working hard, and therefore enjoying the satisfaction of a job well done, an achievement attained, or a qualification gained. But when does our innate desire to be productive become a more damaging drive, leading us to struggle and strive beyond what God would ask of us?

One sign that we are striving more than thriving is that we find ourselves propelled by trying to *prove* something to somebody. There have been times in my life when I have realized that my need to succeed is in fact a deep desire to show somebody that I am good enough. Or maybe I work extra hard because somebody has said I cannot do something and so I become determined to prove that I can! This is crazy-making behaviour, and yet so much of what we communicate over social media or coffee is little more than a reinforcement to ourselves and to others that we are, indeed, significant.

Perhaps we strive because we want people to *approve* of us. Many of us are driven by a desire to be liked or to be accepted (not many of us enjoy being disliked!) but until each of us receives a real and personal revelation of the acceptance we have in God – the creator of the universe who not only approves of us, but designed us and loves us unconditionally – we may well be prone to people-pleasing or yearning for the approval of others.

But what if our desire could instead be to *improve*? Could we grasp the potential God has placed in us, and the plans he has for us, and focus on these as our motivation? As we do, we will discover there is a subtle but significant difference between training and trying. I can try hard to run a marathon, but without training I will fall after the first few miles, or even earlier. Likewise, my children are learning the piano, but they can't simply sit down and try to play Beethoven's Moonlight Sonata; they need to train for years, playing those pesky scales again and again before they achieve their goal.

God is passionate about us and wants us to improve our God-given strengths and gifts, but the passage from

1 Timothy reminds us that we should be training ourselves to be godly – not just trying harder to be good or attempting to pray for hours, but training ourselves, one step at a time, to grow in our spiritual strength. This, the writer says, is the thing that we should labour and strive for, and this goal alone will release us to thrive in our various roles, responsibilities and relationships. Or as it says in Matthew 6:33, we should "seek first the kingdom of God and his righteousness, and all these other things will be added" to us (ESV).

SOMETHING TO TRY

Open your diary and review your time allocations, your priorities, and the motivation for what you do. Are there areas or relationships which you would say are driven by a need to prove yourself, a need to seek approval, or do you aim to improve in your calling with God's help?

Consider what practical and spiritual training would help you and plan to start practising the discipline needed in these areas – one day at a time.

SOMETHING TO PRAY

> **Heavenly Father, I thank you that you love me as I am and that you want me to grow and develop without striving unnecessarily. I pray as I seek to train and improve all you have given me, I would avoid the pitfalls of seeking approval or proving myself and that I would seek you first, knowing that you are all I need.**
> **Amen.**

19

EXPECTANCY

GC

Expect great things from God. Attempt great things for God.

William Carey

SOMETHING TO READ

John 6:1–13

SOMETHING TO THINK ABOUT

Can you imagine travelling a long way and then sitting in a field for hours in the heat, feeling hotter and hungrier as time passes, and yet your desire to listen to the man before you is so great that you cannot bring yourself to go in search of food? This is the picture on the hillside that we find in John 6. Five thousand people (minus women and children – who would have taken the head count up as far as 15,000) have travelled a long way across the lake to listen to Jesus. In the midst of this, Jesus effectively turns to his disciples and asks, "Who's got lunch?"

Clearly none of them have any food, so eleven of the disciples do nothing. However, Andrew finds a young boy with a packed lunch and brings it to Jesus. It is hard to believe that a young lad would give his food away – I mean if thirteen years in youth ministry have taught me anything it's that this is something of a miracle! Andrew takes the lunch to Jesus and as good as says, "I don't know what use this is but you're Jesus so I am going to bring it to you anyway!" Jesus then takes the boy's packed lunch and feeds everyone in the field. No one complains about the quality of the lunch and there are twelve basketfuls left over.

For me the miracle of the story is not so much the divine multiplication of the bread and fish (after all Jesus made the fish and the bread in the first place so producing some more was an easy enough task). No, the miracle is that the little boy, and then Andrew, both thought the tiny offering that they had in their hands was worth bringing to Jesus in the first place. Although it was a terribly small offering they were expectant that in the hands of Jesus it could be significant.

Sometimes the biggest barrier to being used by the Lord is the fact that we think we have nothing to offer and therefore don't expect him to use us. The story of the feeding of the five thousand turns such thinking on its head. If the Lord used a little boy's smelly fish and dried bread (that perhaps he didn't fancy eating) to feed a field, what might he do with the little we have?

The Irish eighteenth-century philosopher Edmund Burke said, "Nobody made a greater mistake than he who did nothing because he could only do a little." Let's not be guilty of that. Let's look more positively at what we can bring and be expectant that in the hands of Jesus it could be used immensely. Let's try to be like the little boy who bought his small offering to Jesus, not the thousands who did nothing. Let's be expectant that all we have can be placed in the hands of Jesus and used to do more incredible things than we would ever think possible. After all it is he "who is able to do immeasurably more than all we ask or imagine, according to his power that is at work within us" (Ephesians 3:20).

SOMETHING TO TRY

I've always loved playing football and have often used it to reach others with the gospel. However, in recent times this has slipped a little. About a year ago I asked the Lord to help me reach people through football again. Within a couple of weeks my next-door neighbour was playing for my team and encountering something of Jesus through football. He hasn't become a Christian yet, but he's on a journey and I'm expectant of how the Lord might use me in this small way for his glory.

Think of something in your life that you love doing and ask the Lord to start using that for his glory too. Be expectant that he can use the things you love doing to build his kingdom. He can work through anything!

SOMETHING TO PRAY

> **Lord Jesus, forgive me for when I've not felt significant enough for you to use. Please help me to bring the little I have in my hands to you. I ask you to use it to make a massive difference in the world for your glory. Amen.**

20

DRAWING CLOSER TO GOD
KH

Draw near to God and he will draw near to you.

James 4:8 (RSV)

SOMETHING TO READ

Hide me in the shadow of your wings.

Psalm 17:8

Psalm 17:1–8
Psalm 57

SOMETHING TO THINK ABOUT

As a new parent I was led to believe that our children's lives would be incomplete without the experience of owning a pet. This belief resulted in all kinds of pets taking up residence in our home – the *pièce de résistance* being a leopard gecko that had to be fed live crickets, which in turn had to be fed slices of cucumber. All these animals eventually went the way of all flesh, so in a last attempt to live the good life, we decided to get some chickens. They seemed to be the perfect pets.

The peace and harmony was short-lived, however. One morning, soon after they arrived, we were woken by a great commotion in the yard. Looking out from a bedroom window, we were in time to see an intruder, aka Fantastic Mr Fox. He was quite young, but obviously thought, even so, he could overcome some chicks. We watched helplessly but need not have worried. In an instant, the mother hen reverted to type. Oblivious to her own welfare, she spread her wings wide and the chicks ran to her for cover, drawing close and finding safety and shelter under her wings. She gave the young fox a look as if to say, "Come on! Make my day!" and he sloped away.

A story is told of a farmyard fire that began in a barn but swiftly spread, sweeping through the farmyard itself and causing widespread devastation. The farmer tried to save his livestock, but the hen and her chicks had nowhere to hide and were soon engulfed by the flames. In the early morning, the farmer walked through the yard to see the damage, and his eye fell on the charred remains of the bird. As he stooped to pick up the burnt body, he felt something move. Unbelievably, four little chickens were sheltering underneath her wings – they were still alive! As they had run to her in that time of danger, she had gathered them to her and protected them. It is a beautiful image that Jesus no doubt had in his mind's eye when he looked over the city of Jerusalem: "Jerusalem, Jerusalem… how often I have longed to gather your children together, as a hen gathers her chicks under her wings" (Matthew 23:37).

King David also used this image in the psalms. He was writing at a time of incredible challenge and pressure. He had fought long and hard, he was on the run, and had experienced treachery, betrayal, and disappointment. And in the midst of this hardship he cried out to God, "Hide me in the shadow of your wings, until the disaster has passed." This is not a fighting image – you cannot win battles from this position – but it is a place of peace, of safety, and it is for a season.

I'm sure that you, like me, have experienced those times in your life when you are desperate to hear Jesus say,

"Come apart and rest awhile." It is not so much that we put our feet up – although at such times we would be wise to say no to more things than we normally would. It is more that in our heart and spirit we rest, knowing there is nothing to prove to the one who loves, cherishes, and protects us under his wings.

In the late eighteenth century, a young preacher from Somerset was travelling home through the Mendip Hills when he was caught in a terrible storm. He ran through the driving rain and found shelter in a crevice in the rock. As he pressed into the narrow opening and waited for the storm to pass, he was inspired to write the first line of what has now become the famous hymn "Rock of Ages, cleft for me; let me hide myself in Thee".

The storms of life can come to us out of a bright blue sky. Life can be challenging for all kinds of reasons; church, family, and work are rarely without issues. Whatever your situation today, run to him, take shelter in the shadow of his wings, and rest secure in the place he has there for you – a place that is immeasurably wider, longer, higher, and deeper than you can ever imagine.

SOMETHING TO TRY

Consider what particular challenges you face today, then take a moment to picture God firstly as the mother hen protecting her chicks, and then as the "Rock of Ages" cleft, especially for you. Note down the images, words, or feelings that come to mind.

Choose to draw close to God, to shelter from the storms of life and to enjoy time in his presence.

SOMETHING TO PRAY

Rock of Ages, cleft for me; let me hide myself in Thee. Amen.

21

INTENTIONALITY

RP

A life-changing love is inconvenient.

Tim Keller, "Gospel in Life: Grace Changes Everything", DVD sermon

SOMETHING TO READ

> *So if you're serious about living this new resurrection life with Christ, act like it. Pursue the things over which Christ presides. Don't shuffle along, eyes to the ground, absorbed with the things right in front of you. Look up, and be alert to what is going on around Christ – that's where the action is. See things from his perspective.*
>
> **Colossians 3:1–2 (MSG)**

SOMETHING TO THINK ABOUT

When it comes to thinking about spiritual disciplines, living a life of intentionality rarely makes the list. We typically think of prayer, meditation, service, silence, and other virtuous contemplative acts as the way to go deeper in our relationship with God and his Spirit. However, in today's passage from Colossians, we see Paul addressing the church in Colossae about how to be serious "about living this new resurrection life" that we have inherited because of Jesus... and it involves intentionality. But what exactly do we mean when we talk about living a life of intentionality?

To be intentional about something is to do something on purpose; to be deliberate about it. And according to Jesus, this is exactly what he is after from his followers. Unfortunately, all too often our relationship with Jesus can become compartmentalized and compromised and, consequently, reduced to a one-hour worship session in church on a Sunday. This is the opposite of a life of intentionality. A Jesus-centred life does not merely happen by showing up somewhere once a week, or via osmosis. Instead, it is a wilful decision: to act; to "Pursue the things over which Christ presides"; to look up to what God is doing in our world, begin to see things from his perspective, and then take a step out that puts action to our faith. It has been said that, "Christianity is an exercise of the will" – a wilful engagement that lives a life of purpose.

If you think about it objectively, the only things that are accomplished in life are done so intentionally. Your car payments don't get paid by accident. The airline pilot doesn't magically and inexplicably land at their destination. Jesus didn't sacrifice his life for all of humanity as some sort of strange coincidence. So why do we think that living a life pleasing to God that makes much the gospel is going to just magically happen? It's not, and it is going to take an exercise of the will. In fact, Jesus died so that you could practically and intentionally do something with your faith in your limited time on this planet. It's an invitation, and it is time for his followers to live this out!

SOMETHING TO TRY

How do you practically live out your allegiance to Jesus? What does it look like amid your day-to-day routine? Jesus desires to have access to all areas of your life, not just Sunday mornings.

Today, after you read this, spend some time in prayer asking the Spirit to lead you into an area of your life that needs some attention, to wilfully and deliberately give access for God to move. Write down that area of your life wherever you keep notes (on your phone, journal, etc.) and then spend some deliberate time praying and asking the Spirit to show you how to intentionally engage to bring an overflow of the gospel to this area of your life. It could be something small or something rather life-altering, but whatever the case, your prayer should be to allow the Spirit to move here and then for that movement to translate into action.

SOMETHING TO PRAY

Choose to pray with intentionality today. Pray for your family, neighbours, community, and city. As the Spirit brings each one to mind, simply pray:

> **Father, how can I be a vessel of grace in each one of these areas? What is your perspective on each one of these people, and how can I intentionally live out the gospel to bring your kingdom to them today?**

22
SACRIFICE

CM

Human progress is neither automatic nor inevitable... Every step toward the goal of justice requires sacrifice, suffering, and struggle; the tireless exertions and passionate concern of dedicated individuals.

Martin Luther King Jr

SOMETHING TO READ
John 15:9–13

SOMETHING TO THINK ABOUT
A few months ago we received a surprising and slightly disconcerting phone call from my husband's mother. She informed us that she would soon be going into hospital, which seemed strange, as she is a particularly healthy woman in her seventies. It turned out that the reason for her medical expedition was that she had decided to give away one of her kidneys. This was, as you can imagine, a bit of a shock. She didn't know who it would go to, but she knew she had a kidney "spare" and that it would help somebody tied to a dialysis machine somewhere. The resulting operation cost her physically, and her recovery was slow and painful, but that kidney was successfully transplanted and, as she had hoped, transformed somebody's life.

It shouldn't have surprised us really, as my mother-in-law has made a habit of sacrificing her time, money, and possessions in the hope that they would bring life and hope to others. She only really had her body left to give away! (We have since asked if she could give us a heads up if she plans to give away any other body parts in the future.) The thing is, her faith in Jesus and all he sacrificed for her in his life and in his crucifixion, along with all he gained for her in his resurrection, has shaped the principles of her life, and she fully depends on him to give her what she needs as she gives what she can, and then some.

Sacrificing ourselves for others, for justice, for a cause close to our heart, and for Jesus' calling on our life, always costs us something. If it doesn't, then it isn't actually a sacrifice at all. But who likes making themselves feel uncomfortable? Nobody. I certainly don't, even though I know that it is not always going to be pleasant if I want to do something great. Speaking honestly, although we long to make a difference to our world, we are also people who find it hard to give up cake for a week – so it is a big decision to give up serious time or energy for something which isn't about ourselves.

And yet love is always expressed through sacrifice. A marriage is about constant sacrifice unless we want to live in constant tension. Parenting is about living a life of sacrifice in order to give your children all they need to flourish. But even these can be, in part, self-serving. The question is, how prepared are we to fully lay down our lives for those we know, but also perhaps for those who we will never know, but whose lives could be transformed as we give what we can, and then some?

SOMETHING TO TRY

Think of something you could sacrifice this week/month/year – a food group, a gadget or an amount of time or money, for example. Think carefully.

Now reflect upon your decision – how easy was your choice? Is it a real sacrifice and should you make it cost a little more? And, importantly, would anybody else benefit from your decision? Reconsider if necessary and then joyfully and willingly give to God as he has lavishly given to you.

SOMETHING TO PRAY

Lord, I thank you that you are abundantly generous to me; I have so much around me to be thankful for. I am sorry when I fail to notice your mercies that are new every morning and your constant provision in my life. Thank you, once more, for the sacrifice of Jesus and the love that compelled him to die on a cross, so that I might live. Help me, Lord, to live a life of gratitude but also of sacrifice, so that through my life, others might live more fully and your kingdom might come here on earth as it is in heaven.

I place my life into your hands.

Amen.

23

RESURRECTION

Jesus' resurrection is the beginning of God's new project not to snatch people away from earth to heaven, but to colonize earth with the life of heaven. That, after all, is what the Lord's Prayer is about.

N. T. Wright, *Surprised by Hope*

SOMETHING TO READ

He was supreme in the beginning and – leading the resurrection parade – he is supreme in the end. From beginning to end he's there, towering far above everything, everyone. So spacious is he, so roomy, that everything of God finds its proper place in him without crowding. Not only that, but all the broken and dislocated pieces of the universe – people and things, animals and atoms – get properly fixed and fit together in vibrant harmonies, all because of his death, his blood that poured down from the cross.

Colossians 1:18–20 (MSG)

SOMETHING TO THINK ABOUT

I was sitting with Mark who had been addicted to cocaine and heroin for many years. I had got to know him over the last few years and he was a lovely guy, but very messed up. A little while ago I was with him because he had just had another relapse after being clean for a year. In desperation he had jumped in his car to buy some cocaine and while under the influence he had driven home. Missing the gateway, Mark had driven into the wall and found himself in a battered mess.

I sat with Mark and talked about life. The man beside me was just about physically alive, but he was spiritually dead. Mark might have had a pulse but he was certainly somewhere else. You might say someone was in but the lights weren't on. It's possible for us to look at people like Mark and say, "I'm not as bad as that." Reality check: we aren't graded on the behaviour of others, we aren't ranked against other people, we are held up against Jesus. No matter what angle you look from, when we're up against Jesus we just don't make the grade.

Jesus had this idea that it was possible to be physically alive but still be dead on the inside. This is why he says in the story of the prodigal son, "Your brother was dead, but is alive again!" When a young man says he wants to follow Jesus but first needs to go and bury his father, Jesus responds, "Let the dead bury the dead." Unless you have seen zombies burying zombies or dead boys walking then we have to presume Jesus is talking about something else.

We can sometimes think the "good news" is about bad people becoming good people – it's not. The "good news" is about dead people becoming living people. There is nothing more rebellious than Jesus' resurrection because it refuses to accept the world as it is. Jesus' resurrection challenges everything we think to be true and proclaims that God hasn't finished with the world.

The beauty of Jesus' resurrection is that it didn't just happen, it *happens*. This resurrection happens every day in the lives of people who choose to accept that Jesus is the answer.

Mark got on his knees the afternoon that I met him and he sobbed and shook and cried out to Jesus. Mark's prayer was so simple, "Help!" From this moment those of us that know him started to see the resurrection Spirit at work in him and he is again celebrating being clean for a year.

SOMETHING TO TRY

Take some time to pray and rejoice where God has been involved in resurrection in your life. Who were you before you fully engaged with Jesus? Where were you dead but now alive? Who are you now becoming because of this? Take time to be thankful and pray for those who you know that need to experience this same resurrection power for themselves.

SOMETHING TO PRAY

Oh Risen Lord
Be to me your resurrection and life
Be resurrection to me when I'm caught in the grip of sin and shame
Be resurrection when I don't believe and trust in you
Be resurrection to me when I don't live as you invite me to
Be resurrection in my darkest place and in my lightest place
Be resurrection in my life when sickness has a grip
Be resurrection in my broken relationships
And be resurrection to me when words spoken over me cripple and distort your image in my creation.

24

LEADING INTO DEEPER

KH

... let us consider how we may spur one another on toward love and good deeds.

Hebrews 10:24 (TNIV)

SOMETHING TO READ

John 1:35–44
John 6:8–9
John 12:22

SOMETHING TO THINK ABOUT

When I am speaking at a meeting, I sometimes ask the audience to raise their hands to vote for their favourite disciple. There are quite a lot of people who vote for John, but Peter always wins. I think it's because he seems so much like us – one minute promising to die for Jesus, the next denying him. There is normally a maverick who will raise their hand for Thaddeus, but I think my choice would be the same as the few who seem drawn to Andrew.

It was Andrew who introduced Peter to Jesus (John 1:40–42); it was Andrew who introduced the boy with the loaves and fish to Jesus (John 6:8–9); and it was Andrew who tried to get some Greek people an audience with Jesus (John 12:20–22). Andrew is rarely centre stage, but he seems to genuinely want people to get to know Jesus a little better. It is a lovely quality to have.

In my first year as an undergraduate I remember being involved on the planning committee of the university mission. At one of the initial meetings, we were all issued with a piece of paper and asked to write down the names of five people we would invite to an evangelistic supper. As I picked up my pen I remember wondering whether my desire was truly that people would come to know Jesus, or whether I simply wanted to tick the right boxes and be seen to be doing the right thing. Later in life, I quickly discovered that there is no shortage of people who will give you their theological opinion, put you right on any number of issues, or dispense advice like some guru slot machine, but to find someone whose genuine aim is that you would know Jesus more deeply – that really is to find a treasure.

I will sit through an entire conference for the sake of one good idea – one inspired nugget of wisdom. Some years ago, a phrase from a seminar speaker made me sit up and listen. The speaker said, "Everyone needs three people in their lives: a Timothy to pass the faith on to; a Barnabas to encourage them; and a Paul to mentor them." As I listened, I began to think about my own life. I had some Timothys – people whose lives had crossed my path and who I had been able to influence in their journey of faith. I had some wonderful Barnabas figures who encouraged me to keep going in the faith. But then I wondered, "Do I have a Paul(ine!)?" I didn't. I was busy. I was immersed in family life and in Christian ministry, but I really didn't have anybody who saw part of their life's work as leading me into a deeper relationship with Jesus.

Not long after, I found my "Pauline". I meet with Annie on a regular basis. We pray together, and we share together. I know that she is "for" me, and the safety of that means that when we meet I can let down my guard and be honest and vulnerable. She is someone who is not afraid to "speak the truth in love". On many occasions she has challenged me and spoken directly into my life. When I am feeling insecure she reminds me of my true identity and who it is that God has called me to be. She reminds me of his good plans and purposes for me and of his faithfulness, and in doing that she leads me into a deeper relationship with God. It is as if she is my "Andrew" and says to me, "Katharine, there is someone I would like you to get to know better. His name is Jesus."

Of course, I want somebody to help me be a better communicator, a more effective leader, and a better writer, but deep in my heart I know that none of that is anywhere near enough. I need somebody to lead me not just into "better", but into "deeper". Immeasurably deeper. I need my "Paul".

SOMETHING TO TRY

Everyone needs three people in their lives: a Timothy to pass the faith on to; a Barnabas to encourage them; and a Paul to mentor them.

To whom can you be:
- *a Timothy*
- *a Barnabas*
- *a Paul?*

Take steps this week to make contact with them, and then to pass on a word of encouragement or challenge that will lead them into knowing Jesus more deeply.

SOMETHING TO PRAY

Think of the person/people that you have identified. Use Paul's prayer for the Philippians to pray for them.

> **And this is my prayer: that your love may abound more and more in knowledge and depth of insight, so that you may be able to discern what is best and may be pure and blameless until the day of Christ, filled with the fruit of righteousness that comes through Jesus Christ – to the glory and praise of God. [Amen.]**
>
> **Philippians 1:9–11**

25

LISTENING (TO GOD AND OTHERS)

MP

Jesus called the crowd to him and said, "Listen and understand."

Matthew 15:10

SOMETHING TO READ

> *The first service that one owes to others in the fellowship consists in listening to them. Just as love to God begins with listening to His Word, so the beginning of love for the brethren is learning to listen to them.*
>
> **Dietrich Bonhoeffer, *Life Together***

SOMETHING TO THINK ABOUT

Listening can easily be misconstrued as praying. Listening is what happens before prayer. It is a necessary prelude to intercession. This is true in the earthly, human realm where you need to engage others around you and hear their hearts before you can adequately intercede for them. We cannot pray for someone if we have not first listened to their request. The same is true in the heavenly, spiritual realm when you bring requests before Jesus. We cannot pray to the Father without first listening to the guidance of the Holy Spirit. If we jump into a prayer without first listening, we are bound to miss some of what God would have for us as we encounter him in intercessory prayer! (Let us also not forget that his voice might be silent if we have not given ourselves over to him in confession.)

Our salvation was established securely through listening to God's voice and then heeding it (Ephesians 1:13). Without listening to the voice of the Lord calling us into the fold, we would still be lost and wandering away, feeling the sense of the loneliness that came from our God-shaped void. If we come into relationship with God through hearing, we must be mindful that this is an extremely important skill that we can develop to serve the world around us, for the sake of God's kingdom. Listening is not merely a skill for trained professionals in a counselling room. It must become a vital attribute of the people of God, rooted in holy and sincere practices of patience and compassion. This is, after all, what was modelled by Jesus. He made time to listen to others, and in turn, they listened to him, and many received his life-changing invitations.

Impatient, half-hearted listening could be the very thing that drives a wedge into your relationships. It is also, quite possibly, the very thing that hinders evangelism efforts. Most importantly, that kind of listening is a component in a mediocre relationship with God.

Taking time to listen, giving our full attention to the one with whom we're communicating, is hugely beneficial for both parties. So it makes more than a little sense to keep practising the art of mouth shut, ears open.

SOMETHING TO TRY

We let our chaotic circumstances dictate the level of engagement we give to others. However, the biggest component to listening well to God and to others is to be very present in the moment. You can start small by aiming to do this in short exercises with a co-worker, a child, a friend, or a spouse. Let them speak without you first thinking about how you are going to respond. Be sure to hear everything they say and be slow to speak. Then, as an act of active listening, repeat back what you heard before giving advice or solutions.

SOMETHING TO PRAY

Every character in the Old and New Testament who did great things for God, did them because they heard from God first. When engaging God in prayer, spend a few minutes in silence first, waiting to hear from God before you bring your intercession. Place your heart in a posture of humility.

Simply begin by asking, "Lord, is there anything you want to say to me?"

26

ASKING

CM

If you remain in me and my words remain in you, ask whatever you wish, and it will be done for you.

John 15:7 (TNIV)

SOMETHING TO READ

Luke 11:1–11

SOMETHING TO THINK ABOUT

I clearly remember when my children were toddlers, or "threenagers" as I called them. Every day they woke up with an apparently endless amount of energy, and a constant curiosity about the world, leading to a thousand questions beginning with the word "Why?" One day, while walking along the local seafront, my daughter looked at the construction equipment and said, "Why is the crane blue?" Now she is a teenager and we still ask her why cranes are particular colours and I think, deep down, she finds us hilarious.

Children have no self-consciousness whatsoever about asking questions, or asking for more, or asking for what they want. They assume that everybody is there to fulfil their wishes. And while, as we grow up, most of us learn that we are not the centre of the universe, the sad part is that we also often stop asking about anything. We don't like asking for information or for help and sometimes we don't like to bother God, either. Perhaps we don't want to look unintelligent or vulnerable to others, or to sound as if we are moaning.

One of the blessings we have discovered as a result of my husband losing his sight has been learning to ask all over again. I have asked God a lot of questions, and I have asked God for a lot of help. I have even reverted to asking "Why?" from time to time. We have also asked people for all kinds of help, from driving to DIY, and discovered friendship and kindness we would never have experienced if we had not needed to be so vulnerable.

Wouldn't it be great if our church communities were always places where we felt free to ask? Every member of God's family has something to give, but we also all have our own needs. We should be defined by the way we love each other (John 13:35), meeting each other's practical, emotional, and spiritual needs. But the release of blessing only happens when one person asks another how they are or when somebody steps out and asks for prayer, or asks for help.

Most importantly, as individuals and as the family of God, we must never grow out of asking God to be involved with our lives and our world. He longs for us to be persistent in prayer, bringing our concerns and desires and questions to him. James 1:5 tells us, "If any of you lacks wisdom, you should ask God, who gives generously to all without finding fault, and it will be given to you" (TNIV). Do you have anything happening in your life where you could use the wisdom of God? Ask God about it!

As we ask others and ask God, we should remember that we have a relationship with our heavenly Father, and he asks us questions too. From the Garden of Eden where he asks Adam and Eve, "Where are you?" to when Jesus asks the disciples "Will you follow me?" God reminds us that he is not some kind of heavenly slot machine, simply there to meet our every need. He wants us to remain in him, and for him to remain or abide in us, asking and answering in the context of a relationship of mutual trust.

SOMETHING TO TRY

Do you find it easier to ask questions or to give answers?

Today, try asking more questions. Ask others how they are or what they mean. Ask for more information. Ask God about all you are involved with or the concerns on your heart. Make a note or journal about what you learn from asking more.

SOMETHING TO PRAY

Heavenly Father, thank you that you ask me to follow you.

Help me to be a person who asks for help, who asks after others and who asks you to be involved in all I do.

Lord, help me to listen attentively, expectant for your wisdom and your provision.

In Jesus' name. Amen.

27

THANKFULNESS

AG

Bless the Lord, O my soul, and all that is within me, bless his holy name.
Bless the Lord, O my soul, and do not forget all his benefits...

Psalm 103:1–2 (NRSV)

SOMETHING TO READ

Psalm 103:1–22

SOMETHING TO THINK ABOUT

"Bless the Lord" is something the psalmists command their souls to do with great passion and regularity.

> To bless God means to recognize his great richness, strength, and gracious bounty and to express our gratitude and delight in seeing and experiencing it.
>
> **John Piper, *What Does it Mean to Bless God?*,**
> **desiringgod.org**

When I lived in London I found that commuting did not result in exhorting my soul to bless the Lord. More often than not my soul wanted to crush and destroy all in its warpath. I decided change was necessary and determined to use my cycle ride each morning as a journey of thankfulness. It was transformative to my journey, my day and, I would go as far as to say, my life. My attitude was altered by it, and in turn my character benefitted. So did those around me.

Using all my senses, and with all the thoughts of the day in my mind, I would thank God for the greatness of all his work, allowing my surroundings to trigger a flow of thought. "Thank you Lord for the way clouds are always changing, for the smell of roofer's tarmac, thank you for balance and the ability in my legs to cycle, for Debs who gave me this bike, for the invention of the wheel and the way it has changed the world."

A bus passes just a little too close. "Thank you Lord for cycle helmets, and the minds of the engineers who design them."

I pull up at the lights alongside the hospital. "Thank you Lord for those who give their lives and efforts to care for others." I pull away. "Thank you for the joy of the wind on my face, for the housemate who made me smile this morning, for the clothes on my back and the food in my tummy, for the person who grew and picked my banana, for the transport system that means I can enjoy bananas. Thank you for the job I'm going to, for the people in my life today."

The longer you go on, the more you find to be grateful for – you don't have to think, just realize. This world is full of delight and all of it from the Father's hand. Thanking him for it draws him into my enjoyment of it and makes me more aware of his presence.

Recently there's been a flurry of Facebook activity about finding three things to be thankful for each day. If I can only find three then I have a problem. I now drive to work along country roads. It's less agro-inducing, but I still try to maintain the thankfulness practice a couple of times a week. As I fill my twenty-minute journey with things I'm grateful for, I feel the joy of God's Spirit in me and with me – it's like we're taking delight in the world together. Taking the time to find and acknowledge the myriad things I have to be thankful for takes my eyes off me and turns them to the Creator. It humbles me to actually say thank you, rather than taking them for granted or assuming God knows I'm grateful. So I will encourage my soul to bless the Lord, and feel the delight of his Spirit in my appreciation of his goodness.

SOMETHING TO TRY

If you have to travel anywhere today, even a walk to the post box, make it a journey of thankfulness. Allow your mind to explore the things around you that God has made and impacted. If you're staying put, try it while looking out of the window for five minutes, in the shower or even sitting on the toilet. There is nowhere that God hasn't provided things that benefit you. Make your gratitude journey a regular habit for a few weeks and consider the change in the experience or in you.

SOMETHING TO PRAY

Thank you God. Thank you, thank you, thank you. For this, for that, for him, for her, for here, for now, for you. Thank you and thank you.

28

CELEBRATION

MGu

The kingdom of God is a party for a bunch of people with whom we wouldn't be caught dead spending a Saturday night, had we not also been invited.

William H. Willimon and Stanley Hauerwas, *Lord, Teach Us*

SOMETHING TO READ

1 Chronicles 15:25–29

SOMETHING TO THINK ABOUT

If I were to ask you to name the spiritual disciplines, I suspect celebration wouldn't be one of them. It's just not hair shirt enough – despite the fact that someone has to clean the fudge cake out of the carpet, and that's a real act of service. But celebration was certainly a habit for Jesus – who isn't nearly as dour as we sometimes portray him.

In fact, in the Old Testament celebration is a way of life. God repeatedly tells his people to rejoice on their many festivals. It's not an optional extra. It's a command. The word for rejoice here is *simcha*, the Hebrew for party. "You will party."

And Jesus did. Three times a year he went up to Jerusalem from Galilee, a three-day journey on foot. Passover, Pentecost, and Tabernacles. The pilgrim festivals lasted eight days and were a heady integration of worship, procession, dance, storytelling, good food, new wine, and fun. His life was a round of communal merriment and joy in homes as well as the Temple.

For us, real celebration isn't an excuse for a knees-up, or standing around spraying each other with Pringles! It can mean going immeasurably deeper into worship, as we give ourselves to God, body, mind, and spirit, lavishing time on him, a great gift when we have so little of it. "The joy of our Lord should oil the wheels of our obedience," said Matthew Henry, the great eighteenth-century Bible commentator. It's an offering that's a painful sacrifice for anyone in grief or depression. And God sees that and welcomes it for what it is. There were Jews who danced in Auschwitz on the feast of the giving of the law in obedience to the commandment to rejoice on your festival. Michal, King David's wife, despised her husband for abandoning his dignity in God's presence. And was sterile ever after. Is it surprising that the church that suffers most and grows the fastest – the African church – has the most to show us about celebration?

Celebration can be witness as well as worship. When the philosopher Nietzsche was asked why he was so hostile to Christianity, he said, "I never saw the members of my father's church enjoying themselves." This from a philosopher whose ideology later had a great influence on Nazism, which in turn caused so much death and destruction – perhaps an untold destructive impact from the want of a bit of joy. The church has lost almost an entire generation. We bored our children out of the doors and now need a dramatic rethink.

I invited my friend Bev to see a theatre company perform a Christmas comedy at our church. Someone laid on mulled wine and mince pies and, as she imbibed, Bev looked round and said wistfully, "What I'd give to be part of a community like this." She is now. Witnessing isn't threatening for a community celebrating together. "Joy is the net of love by which we catch souls," said Mother Teresa.

The Hebrew word for festivals is *moedim*, which also means "rehearsals". Authentic celebration is also prophetic – a rehearsal for the great banquet in the kingdom when all tears and heartaches, every injustice and suffering, will disappear in God's eternal presence. So it tells a world where people binge-drink to escape bad news and hopelessness, relentless stress and intense loneliness; that no matter how it seems, God is on the throne and all is well. And the watching world will decide whether that kingdom is what it wants by what they see in us.

SOMETHING TO TRY

Henri Nouwen defined celebration as a chance to demonstrate our gratitude for the beauty of the life we have been given. Each moment, every day, each birthday, wedding, anniversary or festival, is unique and will never come again. How will you use your next "occasion" for hospitality, worship, and witness?

SOMETHING TO PRAY

Lord, let my life, and the life of my church, be a celebration of your love, and a demonstration of the joy of your eternal kingdom.

29

DISAPPOINTMENT

CM

Blessed is he who expects nothing, for he shall never be disappointed.

Alexander Pope

SOMETHING TO READ

> *I heard and my heart pounded, my lips quivered at the sound; decay crept into my bones, and my legs trembled. Yet I will wait patiently for the day of calamity to come on the nation invading us. Though the fig tree does not bud and there are no grapes on the vines, though the olive crop fails and the fields produce no food, though there are no sheep in the pen and no cattle in the stalls, yet I will rejoice in the Lord, I will be joyful in God my Saviour. The Sovereign Lord is my strength; he makes my feet like the feet of a deer, he enables me to go on the heights.*
>
> **Habakkuk 3:16–19**

SOMETHING TO THINK ABOUT

One of the hardest things about being a parent is watching your children deal with disappointment. Honestly, I would love it if they could learn everything the easy way, but I know that they can't. It hurts me watching them hurt when the guinea pig has died, the homework doesn't get the expected grade, or they are not invited to a particular party. I especially recall the disappointment we felt when, a few years ago, my daughter who studied extremely hard and who spent innumerable hours representing the school with music, failed in her application to become a prefect. Not only that, but most of her friends succeeded and it was tough for her to bear. Everything in me wanted to rush in to that school and solve it for her. And perhaps I could have; I know plenty of mums who certainly would have. But I knew that learning to bounce back from disappointment is perhaps one of the most important parts of our education as human beings, because disappointment cannot always be avoided or negotiated away.

We might as well face it: if we step out and try to do anything significant with our life, we will hit some brick walls along the way. If we invest any amount of time and effort into a relationship, we will, at some point, feel let down. And if, in order to avoid such disappointment, we choose to stay in our house alone forever with the TV and a cat for company, the sad truth is that we will disappoint ourselves! Without wishing to become the prophet that is Eeyore, the unmistakable truth is that we will inevitably feel disappointed at times: forever-friends turn out to be temporary; helpful colleagues are actually serving themselves; family members make decisions that break our hearts; and God does not always answer our prayers as we hoped he would.

So, if disappointment is not surprising, why are we so surprised when it happens? The question is not whether we will ever experience disappointment; the question is how we respond to it. Are we resilient enough to keep going even when we hit life's obstacles or do we crumble in self-pity or blame others for our pain?

God never promised us that life would be easy, but the good news is that he has given us limitless resources in him so that we will know that it is not our strength or power which picks us up and gives us hope, it is him living in us. Paul says to the Corinthians in his second letter, 4:8–9 "we are afflicted in every way, but not crushed; perplexed, but not despairing; persecuted but not forsaken; struck down, but not destroyed" (NASB).

Instead of internalizing disappointment, we can view it with God's help as an opportunity to learn and to grow more dependent upon him as well as seeing more clearly the value of the friends and family he has given us. By faith, we can hang onto the promises of God and remember again the undeniable truth that he *alone* is our rock and our fortress. The world and everybody in it may be less than perfect, but God will never let us down.

SOMETHING TO TRY

Consider a disappointment you are currently dealing with. Write down three ways in which you hope to cope and then bounce back from this current disappointment. Ask God how he might give you the resources you need for what you are facing. Consider asking other faith-filled friends to help you seek God and to believe with you for your three desired outcomes.

SOMETHING TO PRAY

Thank you, heavenly Father, that you have my future in your hands. I thank you that you are faithful whatever my circumstances and that you are with me even as I deal with disappointments.

I pray you would use all things to grow my faith, my compassion and my resilience so that you might be clearly seen in my life. I put my trust in you. Amen.

30

HOPE

**Now faith is being sure of what we hope for and certain of
what we do not see.**

Hebrews 11:1

SOMETHING TO READ

> *The fundamental fact of existence is that this trust
> in God, this faith, is the firm foundation under
> everything that makes life worth living. It's our
> handle on what we can't see. The act of faith is
> what distinguished our ancestors, set them above
> the crowd.*

Hebrews 11:1–2 (MSG)

SOMETHING TO THINK ABOUT

There is a vast difference between the secular definition of
"hope" and the Christian one. For the world, "hope" is typically
distinguished from certainty. "I'm not sure if that is going to
happen or not, but I sure do *hope* it will." But in the Christian
sense of the word, "hope" is so much more. According to the
Bible, "hope" is trusting in a promise that God has given, and
trusting that it shall come to pass. It is trusting God for what
he has already promised and living accordingly. It is living with
confidence that God will not default on what he has promised.

In 1 Peter 1:13, Peter tells believers to, "get your minds ready for action by being fully sober, and set your hope completely on the grace that will be brought to you when Jesus Christ is revealed" (NET). Peter speaks with confidence that this grace will most assuredly be brought to us when Christ is revealed. There is no doubt in his statement. There is no perhaps. There is absolute confidence. This is biblical hope. And for the believer, there is a strong relation between faith and hope. Hope is faith in the future tense.

The writers of the Old and New Testaments lived and wrote with a hope that all that God has said he would do, he actually would. Some might call this childlike faith, others blind faith, some even naivety, but time and time again God delivered on his promises. There was reason for hope. He always came through.

Now, I realize that you are not Peter, you aren't Mary or Martha, or even one of the members of the early church, but you *are* a child of God who has been promised much. In fact, out of all of the people on the planet right now, we (believers) are the only people alive who have reason to hope. For we have been given promises, we have been told what is to happen in the future, and the God of the universe has included us in his ultimate plan of history. This is the firm foundation under everything that makes life worth living.

This truth makes holding onto hope true and right. Faith and hope in our Lord and Saviour must become the anchor for our souls.

SOMETHING TO TRY

What do you hope for? What promises do you believe will come to fruition in your life today?

The natural human tendency is to look at the circumstances that directly affect us today and allow those to dictate how we live. But, to truly live out faith and hope in the One who is bigger is to claim something greater over your circumstances. It is to look to the promises, to allow them to anchor your soul, and to hope in what God has said that is rooted in the work of Jesus.

"Get your minds ready for action... set your hope completely on the grace that will be brought to you when Jesus Christ is revealed" (1 Peter 1:13, NET). Spend some time meditating on these words. Read them multiple times and ask the Spirit to reveal to you specific ways in which you can put these two things into practice. What does this look like for you today in the specific situations and circumstances in which you find yourself?

SOMETHING TO PRAY

> O Lord, in Whom is our hope, remove far from us, we pray Thee, empty hopes and presumptuous confidence. Make our hearts so right with Thy most holy and loving heart, that hoping in Thee we may do good; until that day when faith and hope shall be abolished by sight and possession, and love shall be all in all.
>
> Christina G. Rossetti (1830–94), "Prayer of Hope"

31

HEAVEN ON EARTH

DT

Aim at Heaven and you will get earth "thrown in": aim at earth and you will get neither.

C. S. Lewis, *Mere Christianity*

SOMETHING TO READ

Genesis 1 and 2

SOMETHING TO THINK ABOUT

Heaven on earth is our most compelling reason to get out of bed in the morning, even when it's cold, raining, and the calendar for the day looks dull. Jesus has a mandate for those who choose to believe in him, the same mandate that Jesus lived by – a life lived with our eyes fixed on heaven.

Jesus focused on heaven – not the heaven that looks like clouds, endless singing and cherubs wafting overhead – but something much more tangible. His focus on heaven was an active pursuit of God's restoration plan, bringing what was broken in Genesis 3 back into perfection. Jesus lived as though every moment was an opportunity to haul the hope of heaven into the present.

We believe that, one day, God's glory and full restoration will come about; the book of Revelation is the restoration of Genesis 1 and 2. A day is coming when there are no longer any tears, no more pain, no more fear or injustice, but instead full restoration of God's position as Lord over all things, and our hope, joy, peace, and love before him. Until that day, we get to be like Jesus and take every opportunity to haul glimpses of the heaven to come, into our present.

We saw Jesus pursuing heaven on earth when he stood in front of the men about to stone a woman caught in adultery and said, "Let he who is without sin cast the first stone" (John 8:7, my paraphrase). Jesus didn't avoid the difficult places or the difficult conversations but used every opportunity to bring a glimpse of heaven, of equality. When Jesus made the blind man see, he was taking ordinary life and bringing glimpses of heaven. People would have passed that man every day and never stopped to do or say anything. Jesus takes an ordinary moment and refuses to pass without bringing a bit of heaven to earth.

As Jesus' followers we are called to that same mandate – to bring glimpses of what we know is to come: peace, hope, justice, dignity, joy, and comfort. This is a lifestyle choice, it is a decision for our ordinary everyday to look different. It is an active stepping-in to a different way of life that should be inconvenient to us – we choose not to walk past someone but to stop and give of our time. It compels us towards conversation that promotes love and peace. This lifestyle choice nurtures an expectant heart, where we pray and expect that God will answer prayer, expect that he will restore relationships, heal the sick, set people free and feed the hungry. It leads us to challenge injustice wherever we see it; in the workplace, in the news, in the stuff of our lives.

We have the very best reason to get out of bed in the morning. If we fix our eyes on Jesus and on heaven, we get to be part of something worth living for. Let's not have our eyes fixed on earthly things, but instead let's increase our capacity to see God at work. More than that... let's not just watch what God is doing; let's say "yes" to bringing heaven to earth with him.

SOMETHING TO TRY

Tomorrow is made up of the lifestyle choices of today. What is it that you're hoping for in our future, when heaven comes about? Today why not take some time out of busy life to reflect and think about how your lifestyle is pointing towards heaven and bringing glimpses of heaven to earth?

Grab some space, a pen, and some paper, then reflect on the questions below:

- *What am I most excited about experiencing when Jesus comes back and restores everything to perfection?*
- *What do I come across in my daily life that clashes with the thoughts I just wrote down?*
- *What can I do differently to bring glimpses of heaven on earth to those places?*
- *How will I start?*

SOMETHING TO PRAY

Lord, thank you that we have a great, sure, and certain hope in you.

Jesus, take our everyday ordinary lives and help us give them to you in a sacrifice of praise, expectant that you will use us for your glory. We will no longer walk past, get too busy, or confuse our priorities but instead we will join in with your restoration plan and bring heaven to earth. We long to be imitators of you, so please take our normal lives and help us to live differently.

Amen.

32

GRIEF

AG

All the days ordained for me were written in your book before one of them came to be.

Psalm 139:16b

SOMETHING TO READ

1 Thessalonians 4:13–18

SOMETHING TO THINK ABOUT

In my time at drama school, a TV director wanted us to learn what real emotion looks like on screen. She began asking personal questions with a camera rolling. I was scared – what might I be asked to bare? My turn. "What's the most precious thing you've ever lost?" I thought for a moment. "I'm far too organized to lose *things*. The most important thing I lost was a person." It was an unexpected but honest answer. My course-mates listened with rapt attention as I described learning to carry my own grief and that of those around me.

We're made for eternity. We struggle with the idea that we, or those we love, will not be here forever. The loss of someone's earthly presence, particularly when it happens younger than we think it should, is painful beyond expression.

To purposefully crash metaphors, grief is a mixed bag on a roller coaster. Emotions get messy. This is true and applicable to whatever we are grieving: the loss of a life; a dating or marriage relationship; a friendship; a job or specific role; a health diagnosis; the potential for a child. We have to allow space for mourning all that was or could have been. If we ignore the reality and strength of the feelings, we suffer more.

I shouted at God, I wailed until my face was swollen and my voice was hoarse, I pounded my fists in the pillow like a child. I discovered, each time the storm stilled, that a peace would wash in, in greater waves than the time before. I didn't have to ask God for it, he was there, ready and waiting to blow the soothing of his Spirit, each time I had expressed my anger and sadness.

I learned that everything that comes with grief – the emotions and struggles – is an opportunity to welcome the Spirit more deeply. In these moments, we can know him in the places where we rage about and ache with hurt, injustice, loss, and lack. I experienced the sustaining of the Spirit through experiences I would rather have avoided. I couldn't run away. I couldn't go around. I had to sit in it. The only option was to invite God into it; without him it was too desolate. I won't say it made the process pass more quickly or less painfully. But I will say that I grew as a person – far beyond my own capacity. I've heard it said that grief doesn't get any smaller – the loss will always be there – but we get bigger. As we grow, the grief gets smaller in relation to us, and does not overwhelm us forever.

There's a Latin proverb – *dum spiro, spero* – "As long as I breathe, I hope." Whatever we face, if we are alive there is a glimmer of hope, however dim or faltering. The Holy Spirit sustains us by bringing hope when it feels hopeless. He whispers that there is light in the tunnel, even when we can't see. He coaxes us around another corner. He puts others in our path to support us, to share in our disappointment, to help us through another day while we grow large enough to hold our grief rather than drowning in it.

SOMETHING TO TRY

- *Be a support to the grieving – it's OK to say, "I don't have anything helpful to say, I know this sucks, I'm here." You don't need to offer advice. Be there to listen, pray from a distance, and offer practical help. Grieving people are often unable to face daily tasks; you can do their shopping, wash their dishes, deliver a meal, or clean their house, without being asked or thanked.*

- *When it's your turn – allow every flavour in the soup of your grief to come out. Express your pain to God. Listen and look out for glimpses of hope. Enjoy the waves of peace that come after a storm of emotion.*

- *Think about the times you have experienced grief – try to pinpoint the ways you encountered God in it with you. Consider how you may have grown by going through the situation.*

SOMETHING TO PRAY

Jesus, you said mourners are blessed because they receive your comfort.
Comfort those grieving today.

Thank you for being present in the mess of our pain.
Thank you that you help us grow.

Open our ears and eyes to your Spirit, revealing hope.

33

ANXIETY AND WORRY

RV

Can any one of you by worrying add a single hour to your life?

Matthew 6:27 (TNIV)

SOMETHING TO READ

*Do not be anxious about anything, but in
every situation, by prayer and petition, with
thanksgiving, present your requests to God.
And the peace of God, which transcends all
understanding, will guard your hearts and your
minds in Christ Jesus.*

Philippians 4:6–7 (TNIV)

SOMETHING TO THINK ABOUT

Well, that is easier said than done isn't it?! If you are anything like me, then just reading these verses makes you feel anxious because you worry that you are worrying instead of resting in the peace of God!

Life is often described as being a journey, but in my experience it has been more like a series of stepping stones. The path that my husband, Greg, and I have chosen to walk along has been quite a rocky one, with periods of instability and insecurity (particularly financially) and it has often felt as if we are brought to settle on a stepping stone for a while, and then called to jump off that one and on to the next one.

The worst bit about that is when you are in mid-air: you have left one stone and not yet quite landed on the next, and there is always a worry – is there actually a stone there for me to land on? I wonder if you have experienced something similar.

I understand things very visually and I want to tell you about two pictures that God has given me. The first was right at the beginning of this path, when I left full-time employment in my late twenties because (and this is the only way to put it) God told me to. I genuinely had no idea what I was going to do and had to trust God that he would bring some work in for me.

I felt a clear sense from God that I was walking into the dark holding a candle. When you walk into a dark room and put the light on, you can see the whole room can't you? But if you walk into the dark with a candle, you can only see a small way in front of you. I felt God saying to me that this is what my path would be like: I wouldn't ever be able to see the whole way ahead, but he would just give me enough light to keep on walking. And he has!

The second picture came during a time of very real insecurity and instability, when Greg and I were leaving a big stepping stone and really didn't know where we would land when we jumped. Greg is great at dealing with these things and really does not worry. In fact, his personality means he enjoys the excitement of not knowing the next step! I couldn't be more different and really struggled to continue to be positive.

I felt like I was being dangled over a huge canyon. I could see the rocks on either side of me, and the valley below a long way down. I was travelling high up, suspended over this valley, frighteningly aware that at any moment I could fall. I lived with this picture of myself for quite a while until, one day, I felt like God told me to look up instead of looking down into the canyon way below. As I did so, I suddenly realized that my arms were being held in the strong grasp of an eagle. Yes, I was flying high over a canyon and, yes, it was a long way down if I fell, but my whole perspective changed as I looked up rather than down, saw the eagle and knew s/he would not let me go.

That is where the peace of God comes from: not necessarily from our situations changing (as much as we sometimes long for that to be the case, and sometimes of course that does happen), but from our perspective on those situations changing, allowing God to help us see where he is present in our situation and to rest in him.

SOMETHING TO TRY

Life may be going well for you and you may not have much to be anxious about. But if you do, take some time now to sit quietly in God's presence. Ask him to show you where he is in the picture of what you are currently going through.

SOMETHING TO PRAY

Sit for five minutes in silence. Don't try to think of or pray for anything in particular, just tell God that you are open to him, and sit, allowing your thoughts to go past you as you do so.

34

WORK

Without work, all life goes rotten. But when work is soulless, life stifles and dies.

Albert Camus

SOMETHING TO READ

May the favour of the Lord our God rest on us;
establish the work of our hands for us – yes,
establish the work of our hands.

Psalm 90:17

SOMETHING TO THINK ABOUT

We all work, whether we have a job or not. And we're meant to. We are meant to be engaged in productive activity that makes God's world a better place to live in. We are meant to be producing products or offering services or doing chores or writing songs that enable people to flourish as whole human beings. We are meant to be providing for ourselves, giving to others, and stewarding our gifts. And we are meant to be doing it for God's glory, with God's help and in his strength.

And that is all the more necessary because work can be hard, frustrating, exhausting, boring, soulless, go terribly wrong, trigger bitter rows, and acidic recriminations – all because we failed to meet a deadline or broke someone's favourite teapot or because we're being exploited.

Indeed, it's sometimes hard to really believe that the King of the Universe is interested in our work, our particular work – this tiny little task, this pan I am scouring, this call I am making, this nut I am tightening – but he is (Colossians 3:23–24), because he is not only the King of the Universe, he's our Father. He is not only interested in how we steward the talents, resources, opportunities, freedoms, power he has given us; he's interested in everything about us because he knitted us together in our mother's womb, and has had his kindly eye on us from our first breath. He's our heavenly Father. And that changes everything.

We don't do our work as zero-hour contracted employees, driven by the dread of a poor performance review, or by the lure of a bigger bonus, we do our work as sons and daughters of the King of the Universe, secure in that status, resourced by his power, and looking forward to his reward.

And so we can bring whatever we do to God: talk to him about it, pray for it, seek his wisdom and his strength in it, and his favour: "May the favour of the Lord our God rest on us; establish the work of our hands for us – yes, establish the work of our hands."

SOMETHING TO TRY

A little exercise. Settle yourself. Ask God to be with you by his Spirit. Imagine for a moment that you have been asked to meet an important visitor and show them round the place you work. You go to meet them outside the entrance or perhaps the front door. When you get there you discover it's Jesus and that he actually wants to show you around. Close your eyes and imagine him doing so. What does he show you?

Where does he go? Where does he linger? Who does he point out or talk to? What does he say?

Reflect and pray about what he's shown you. Share it with someone else.

SOMETHING TO PRAY

Our Father,
who art in heaven,
hallowed be your name
in my heart and in my work,
in this workplace and
among all those who work here.

Your kingdom come,
Your will be done
in this earthly workplace,
as it is so perfectly and swiftly and joyously done
in heaven.

Give us today our daily bread –
all we need for life,
all we need to do this work in your way.

And forgive us our sins –
whether carelessness or half-heartedness, pride or
jealousy, anger or lust, selfishness or lack of love,

As we forgive those we work with who sin against
us.

And lead us not into temptation but deliver us
from the evil one
who is opposed to your rule and the ways of
godly love in this place,
as in every place.

For yours is the kingdom, the power and the glory.

This day and for evermore.

Amen.

35

WORSHIP AS LIFESTYLE

RP

Do you know what I want? I want justice... I want it to roll down like rivers, like a mighty flood. I want righteous actions... like a stream that never dries up. That's what I want. That's all I want.

Amos 5:24 (my paraphrase)

SOMETHING TO READ

> *Therefore, I urge you, brothers, in view of God's mercy, to offer your bodies as living sacrifices, holy and pleasing to God – this is your spiritual act of worship. Do not conform any longer to the pattern of this world, but be transformed by the renewing of your mind. Then you will be able to test and approve what God's will is – his good, pleasing and perfect will.*
>
> **Romans 12:1–2**

Isaiah 58

SOMETHING TO THINK ABOUT

The word "worship" is derived from the Old English verb *weorthscipe*, which means "to ascribe worth" or "to acknowledge the worth" of something. In the Greek, we find the word *proskuneo*, meaning "to fall down". In Hebrew it's *shachah,* meaning "to bow down". To worship something is to acknowledge the worth or value of something, and the act of falling down and bowing before it in reverence.

For the Christian, when it comes to worship, we typically see this idea most lived out in our church services during sung worship. Here we try to focus on the Most High God and sing praises and honour to the only one who is worthy of our praise. We bow in our hearts and minds as we ascribe worth to our Lord and Saviour. But when we begin to examine the apostle Paul's writings on true worship, as seen in our Romans passage today, we find that Paul argues our entire lives can be worship. Not just Sundays and sung worship sessions, but everyday, ordinary, day-to-day life can be done in a way that becomes living worship.

In Eugene Peterson's Message translation of Romans 12:1–2, he has, "Take your everyday, ordinary life – your sleeping, eating, going-to-work, and walking-around life – and place it before God as an offering." This worshipping with your life is what Jesus died for, and what God is after. Yes, sung worship is holy and pleasing to God. Yes, we should continue to give that our all. But, at the end of the day, God wants us to live a whole life of worship. In fact, in this same Romans passage, Paul tells us that our lives can be a living sacrifice, our hearts the altar where we give glory to God. We can – and should – live (because of the cross) in a way that brings glory to God and brings his kingdom to earth.

In Isaiah 58, we find God's people wanting to be close to him, crying out to him, but feeling as though he is treating them unfairly. They fast, pray, and humble themselves, but find that no matter how many "religious" acts they perform, God is still distant. Why? God tells them that although they do all of the "right" things religiously, at the same time they drive their workers too hard, they neglect the down-and-out, they don't allow their worship rituals to translate into their daily lives. God goes on to tell them that what he truly wants from his people is a life of worship that should translate into bringing justice to those in their community. He desires an entire life of worship from his people, not just a ritual or a worship time that happens once a week. God wants all of them, not just a compartment of their lives.

SOMETHING TO TRY

What would it look like for you, your family, or your church to practically live out an Isaiah 58 lifestyle in your community?

What would it look like for you to begin not only going to worship at your church on the weekend, but *living* worship everyday? What would need to shift in the way you view worship and your relationship with God in order for this to take place?

Why not go on a walk and ask the Spirit to open your eyes to how you might live whole-life worship today? Discover ways that you can offer your life as a sacrifice in the way that you serve, love, and go about your ordinary daily life. The opportunities are there, you just need to be awakened to see them through the eyes of the Father. Once you see them, choose to practically do something today about one of the things you are awakened to.

SOMETHING TO PRAY

Lord, open my eyes today to see the world as you do.

May I live and love today the way that I will for eternity with you, and in doing so, may my life be worship to you.

36

SIMPLICITY

DT

Live simply in order that others might simply live.

Attributed to Gandhi

SOMETHING TO READ

Matthew 6:19–24

SOMETHING TO THINK ABOUT

The Bible has a particular way of saying something simple but when we peel the layers back we find it is deeply profound, challenging, and life-changing. Micah 6:8, is a wonderful example of this. "… what does the Lord require of you? To act justly and to love mercy and to walk humbly with your God." This is a deep call to live outside of ourselves and our own bias towards self-interest, and instead to simply live as though God and his people are of paramount importance in our lives. This is not simple at all. In a busy, bustling, impatient world, we quickly lose sight of the dear gift of simplicity.

Interestingly, there are many places throughout Scripture where a word is translated as "simplicity" in some versions and as "integrity" in others. One of my favourite examples of this is 2 Corinthians 1:12. The NIV has: "Now this is our boast: our conscience testifies that we have conducted ourselves in the world, and especially in our relations with you, with *integrity* and godly sincerity. We have done so, relying not on worldly wisdom but on God's grace." The ESV has: "For our boast is this, the testimony of our conscience, that we behaved in the world with *simplicity* and godly sincerity, not by earthly wisdom but by the grace of God, and supremely so toward you." (Italics mine.)

Perhaps in the kingdom of God, simplicity and integrity are woven together as one and the same. Jesus lives a life of compelling simplicity and unswerving integrity. He challenges us that we cannot serve two masters: material wealth and God. This is perhaps the greatest challenge to our discipleship today. Jesus' call to simplicity is a call to complete contentment in him that overflows into every area of our lives: our prayer life, our shopping habits, our go-to when we're feeling low or stressed. All of this should carry the flavour of Jesus, not our favourite TV show, high-street shop, or comfort food.

Jesus' call to simplicity and integrity reveals God's heart for his people.

In pursuit of simplicity, we become true servants: serving one master wholeheartedly and without a second glance elsewhere. We choose integrity in our discipleship.

In pursuit of simplicity, we become loving stewards of our world: choosing an inconvenient way of life in preference of God's creation. We choose integrity in our discipleship.

In pursuit of simplicity, we become authentic worshippers: doing what we say, and saying what we do. We choose integrity in our discipleship.

In pursuit of simplicity, we choose freedom from the chains that bind us as the world tells us to have more, eat more, get more, and keep us from our full potential in Christ. We choose integrity in our discipleship.

In pursuit of simplicity, we make space for others to flourish; we do not live at the expense of others' potential. We choose integrity in our discipleship.

Our simplicity and integrity lead us towards habits and rhythms of life that keep us wholehearted in our focus on the author and perfecter of our faith.

SOMETHING TO TRY

Choose an area of your life that you would like to simplify.

Next choose one small thing you could do differently in service of Jesus.

You might choose to declutter your morning and give yourself fifteen minutes to simply be with Jesus. You could choose to simply recycle everything you can. You might choose to simply buy locally or ethically traded products in order that others might simply live. You might choose to simply ask someone if you can pray for them. Simplicity is not the same as easy. Simplicity is inconvenient but a prize worth fighting for.

SOMETHING TO PRAY

The most simple and profound prayer of Jesus:

> **Our Father in heaven, hallowed be your name,**
> **your kingdom come, your will be done, on earth**
> **as in heaven. Give us today our daily bread.**
> **Forgive us our sins as we forgive those who**
> **sin against us. Lead us not into temptation but**
> **deliver us from evil. For the kingdom, the power,**
> **and the glory are yours, now and for ever. Amen.**

37

GENEROSITY

AG

Freely you have received, freely give.

Matthew 10:8

SOMETHING TO READ

Malachi 3:6–12

SOMETHING TO THINK ABOUT

I was in a fancy-dress shop on a rainy day. A grubby man with a large rucksack walked in and asked the woman at the counter if there were any seconds or leftover hats to give away. He was wet and getting cold. Her tone was incredulous and condescending, "We don't just give hats away."

He must've been desperate if he was willing to consider a fancy-dress second. I ran after him. "Please, can I buy you a hat?" His face lit up. We ducked into a clothes shop along the street and he chose a cap. I inwardly grumbled that being in Brighton's North Laine meant it was more expensive than it needed to be. When he asked what I'd been doing in a fancy-dress shop we embarked on a long conversation about theatre, which, it turned out, we both loved. After a warm and funny chat, I went away feeling I may have entertained an angel unawares. It was worth fifteen minutes and an overpriced hat. My day got sunnier.

Numerous scientific studies have shown that giving money, gifts, and time releases endorphins that make us happier and, indeed, healthier. The Bible says the same. "Test me in this," God challenges the Israelites in Malachi 3, "and see if I will not throw open the floodgates of heaven and pour out so much blessing that there will not be room enough to store it" (Malachi 3:10, TNIV).

The challenge in this passage is to "Bring the full tithe into the storehouse" (NRSV) – to give the first and best 10 per cent of the harvest (not the leftovers) to support those who are full-time ministers, to provide for the widows, orphans, and those unable to work, within the community and beyond.

We can be generous with our money, time, possessions, joy, words of encouragement... all that we have can be shared. There is no reason not to when it clearly blesses us even more than the recipient. Don't worry about mixed motives – just give. Generosity is something we can all be better at – it's a lifestyle we can cultivate. God's Old Testament call to give our first fruits and additional thank offerings, to be hospitable to family, friends and strangers is a baseline. In the New Testament Jesus challenges us to get radical, to lay down everything for others. Sacrificial giving has the potential to be so much more powerful as we make a choice to do without something so that someone else can be provided for.

Our generosity gives the Spirit an excuse or opportunity to get close to us, to give us joy, to tell us something, to let us in on something he is doing. When we give to others, we are giving to God, blessing him by joining his mission. It won't always make us feel instantly closer to God, but with ongoing generosity we will know more of God's heart and grow more like him who gave everything.

"The earth is the Lord's, and everything in it, the world and all who live in it" (Psalm 24:1). If this is true, then making sure everyone has access to the earth's richness should surely be a high priority. And if we know it all belongs to God, we won't struggle so hard to let go.

SOMETHING TO TRY

If you don't plan your monthly giving, set aside some time to work out your take-home pay and what percentage you want to give. If you already do this, look into whether you can spend or save a little less and increase the percentage. Consider your church as a spending priority in local mission, then perhaps something national and global where you feel passionate about joining God's purposes.

Decide now, who are you going to invite for dinner who wouldn't normally get an invitation? Or will you buy lunch or a drink for someone in need? You could give your time and visit someone lonely or volunteer for a community project. Share encouragement by giving someone a compliment or a smile.

When you struggle to give, or worry about having enough left over, remind yourself that it all belongs to God and he will provide for you. Why not try giving more than planned, giving sacrificially, and seeing what the result is?

SOMETHING TO PRAY

> **Lord, everything belongs to you.**
> **Remind me that all I have is yours.**
> **Help me to be more generous every day.**

38

COMMUNITY LIFE

CR

God is not an impersonal thing nor a static thing – not even just one person – but a dynamic pulsating activity, a life, a kind of drama, almost, if you will not think me irreverent, a kind of dance. The pattern of this three-personal life is the great fountain of energy and beauty spurting up at the very centre of reality.

C. S. Lewis, *Mere Christianity*

SOMETHING TO READ

And he said to him, "You shall love the Lord your God with all your heart and with all your soul and with all your mind. This is the great and first commandment. And the second is like it: You shall love your neighbour as yourself. On these two commandments depend all the Law and the Prophets."

Matthew 22:37–40 (esv)

SOMETHING TO THINK ABOUT

I've heard it said by some people that they don't need to go to church to be a Christian. It's true that you can be a Christian and not go to church, but it does make it flipping hard work. What people often mean when they say they don't *need* to go to church is that they don't *want* to go to church. Community life is, in essence, costly. It's costly in time, emotional energy, and in the giving of yourself to it.

The Jesus community that we call "church" isn't a prerequisite for being saved but I would argue that to live a radical, empowered, and discipled life, membership is essential. It is where we can be inspired, equipped, and challenged to grow. At its core, church isn't what you get from it, it's what you give to it. So when you're not at church you might not feel like you're missing out, but you can guarantee that others will miss out on what you have to offer.

Our very understanding of who God is, is directly linked to the way we understand church and community. If the "Creator God", on his own, was the centre of the universe that would mean only power was at the centre of the universe and love could not also take that place. But if God is triune (three in one), then it means that at the centre of all things is a loving relationship. Community life is modelled to us through the relationship between Father, Son, and Holy Spirit.

The Eastern Orthodox Church talks about the Trinity as "perichoresis". This is two Latin words together: *peri* meaning "circular", and *choresis* where we get the word "choreography" or "dance" from. In other words, they say the Trinity is a circular, relational dance with each of the members of the Trinity moving around one another in a beautiful dance. Did you know God loves disco? Each member of the Trinity dances because they love each other so much.

If this is all true, we are able to conclude a few things.

Firstly, if we believe the world was made by a God who is a community of persons who have loved each other for all eternity, and if we believe that we are made in this image, then this means we are created for mutually self-giving love. Love directed any other way, or any self-centredness, destroys the fabric of what God has made in his people.

Secondly, it means that we were created to be involved in the lives of others, and to give of ourselves in a sacrificial, loving way. In other words: it's not enough to invite people to church, we must include people in our lives.

Finally, we can conclude that human existence is about our participation in the life-giving community of the Father, Son, and Holy Spirit. In other words, God says, "Come and dance." We are not made purely to join God in singing, but to join in his dance. He doesn't want religious affiliation, but a life intertwined with his, and consequently with others.

SOMETHING TO TRY

Loving others in a sacrificial way is costly and can hurt us. Try thinking about some of the people you find most difficult to love in your church, or elsewhere. Who do you sit next to each week that you would rather wasn't there because they are difficult? Ask God to allow you to see them as he sees them.

SOMETHING TO PRAY

Father, thank you for inviting me into your dance.

Help me to behave towards others in your Jesus community in the way you have invited me in. Would I not judge, criticize, or condemn but would I invite, love, and encourage. Give me your eyes to see people in the way you do. Let me learn to love like you love, and be slow to judge and quick to affirm.

Finally, Lord, help me to not just invite people into church, but to include them in my life.

Amen.

39

UNITY

RP

Unity in essentials, liberty in non-essentials, charity in all things.
An ancient proverb most famously used by Richard Baxter
(1615–91)

SOMETHING TO READ

John 17:20–26

SOMETHING TO THINK ABOUT

One of the most amazing things about a life in relationship with Jesus is that you aren't alone. Once you enter into a life-altering union with the God of the universe by faith through grace, you are brought into an extended family that spans the globe and history. Your identity changes from a captive of the kingdom of darkness to a saint inheriting the kingdom of light… and you become adopted into a community of others on the same journey.

Before Jesus went through the Passion and was humiliated, ridiculed, tortured, and ultimately murdered on account of us, one of the last things he did on earth was to pray for his followers, present and future. In this "high-priestly prayer", Jesus petitions the Father, "The goal is for all of them to become one heart and mind – just as you, Father, are in me and I in you, so they might be one heart and mind with us. Then the world might believe that you, in fact, sent me" (John 17:21–23, MSG). In other words, "Let them be unified in love!" Jesus states that the goal is unity, just like the unity that Jesus and the Father have. He then goes even further and states that if and when we (believers) attain this, then the outside world (who do not know God) would also believe in him because they see us living this way. Wow, what a testimony that would be to an unbelieving world! They would watch how we live out the radical Jesus lifestyle and in turn believe that the Father had, in fact, sent Jesus. Plainly spoken, our behaviour with one another as followers of Jesus should be a signpost to God for an unbelieving world.

How does this play out in your life?

Historically, one of the issues for the church in the Western world is that we don't always play well together. We tend to get caught up in our differences in the "non-essentials" (as Richard Baxter would put it) to the detriment of a unified church. We are prone to arguing and infighting in the church, and at times, can treat those on the outside with more love and grace than we extend to those on the inside. But according to Jesus, we are all on the same team. You are either on team Jesus or you are not; there is nothing in between.

SOMETHING TO TRY

Today is the perfect day to take a barometer check on how well you are treating your brothers and sisters in Christ. Are you letting petty arguments or differences stand in between you and them? Are you holding a grudge or hanging on to something that is keeping you from living in unity with your eternal family? Is someone's sin against you an anchor to which you are clinging and will not let go?

Might the Spirit be gently nudging you to repent and reconcile?

Allow today to be the day that you initiate the first step towards reconciliation with the one who has hurt you. Follow the example of God who initiated with you (and continues to on a daily basis) to befriend, forgive, overlook, and lie down your agenda for the cause of love and unity of the body. This is the Jesus way of life that the Spirit is leading you into.

Who do you need to speak with today? Who needs to experience the love of Jesus carried through you?

SOMETHING TO PRAY

For the presence of unity where we see it (inspired by Psalm 133):

> **Father God, how good it is when our lives point
> to you.
> When brothers and sisters live together in unity
> It's like an oil of blessing pouring down;
> Spilling out and running over;
> Touching hearts and overcoming hurts.**
>
> **Father God, how good it is when our love for you
> cannot be contained.
> When brothers and sisters love together in unity
> It's like fresh water springs bubbling up;
> Spilling out and running over;
> Inspiring shared vision and overcoming crossed-
> purposes.**
>
> **Father God, we thank you for this sign that you
> are among us by your Spirit.
> As brothers and sisters join together in unity
> It's like a beautiful perfume poured out
> Spilling out and running over;**

**Washing your feet and carrying fragrant worship
to your throne.**

Taken from *Prayers for the Unity of the UK Church –*
Christian Aid Week, 2011. Used with permission from
Christian Aid

40

TRUST

VL

Commit your way to the Lord; trust in him, and he will act.

Psalm 37:5 (NRSV)

SOMETHING TO READ

Psalm 91

SOMETHING TO THINK ABOUT

Trust is a fragile thing: once broken it's hard to repair. Often, it can only truly be repaired through forgiveness and forgiveness is hard. Learning to forgive and trust has been a lesson God has been teaching me for the last two years; a lesson that I am sure will continue for the rest of my life.

It all started when my husband had a heart attack. He had gone into hospital for a relatively routine operation to fix a hole in his heart that he had had from birth. Despite his heart being healthy, apart from the hole, he developed complications a week after the operation and had a massive heart attack that left him "dead" for fourteen minutes. By the grace of God he was still in hospital at the time.

I will never forget the image of my husband in intensive care that night – bloated, almost unrecognizable, and plugged into what seemed like a hundred machines that replaced all the functions of his vital organs. All I could do was put my hand on his shoulder between the wires and pray the only words that would come to me – *Please, God. Help us, help us*. Afterwards, I stood with my children outside the ward and we all held each other in shocked silence.

The consultants had told us that there was no way of knowing if he would recover or if he had received permanent and debilitating brain damage. He was heavily sedated in an induced coma for eleven days and in intensive care for six weeks.

We had to wait and pray.

And I prayed. I prayed day and night, and many others, to whom I am eternally grateful, prayed too. When I laid hands on him in the hospital, in a coma, it felt as if I had been joined by that "great cloud of witnesses" – the many prayers of the saints – as my feeble, broken prayers for healing and recovery were joined with thousands of others. As I prayed, God stirred a deep trust in me that somehow, despite how it seemed, it would all be alright. I had no idea how. But that is the nature of trust.

The day my husband opened his eyes and clearly recognized me and our daughter, we went outside and wept in the waiting room thinking… we'd got him back.

But in reality everything had changed. My husband has made a fantastic, miraculous recovery due to the skill of the medical staff and God's powerful healing; I celebrate his grace and mercy every time I think about it, which is often. But the truth is everything about our marriage and family has changed. This has caused a breakdown of the trust that was based on an old life and a different person from whom my husband had become. God said, at the time of his heart attack, that he would bring things that were hidden into the light and this has been our journey: looking again at each other in a new light, a light formed in the trauma of our experience. This has meant that we have needed and still need to let go of old assumptions and behaviours and embrace a new life. It's like learning to be married all over again after twenty-five years of being together. And I have found that forgiveness is the road we have taken as we journey to a place of restoration. Forgiveness – as well as faith, I am learning – is the seedbed for trust.

SOMETHING TO TRY

Bring to mind any areas of your life where the Holy Spirit is highlighting a breakdown in trust. Carefully and reverently, hold those circumstances and people before God and ask Jesus to help you to forgive.

SOMETHING TO PRAY

> Lord Jesus, you know the secrets of my heart.
> Give me the strength and courage to forgive.
> Catch me, prompt me, when my thoughts or
> behaviour show that I have not forgiven, and
> help me to forgive again.
> Take my un-forgiveness and turn it into trust.
> I trust you, Lord Jesus, to do this.
> Increase my faith in you when I don't know how
> things will go; stir a deep trust in me to rely on
> your grace.
> I ask this in your name.
>
> Amen.

ABOUT THE AUTHORS

Gavin Calver – National Director, British Youth For Christ
www.yfc.co.uk

Mark Greene – Executive Director, London Institute for
Contemporary Christianity
www.licc.org.uk

Abby Guinness – Event Director, Spring Harvest
www.springharvest.org

Michele Guinness – Author and speaker
www.micheleguinness.co.uk

Katharine Hill – UK Director, Care for the Family
www.careforthefamily.org.uk

Krish Kandiah – President, London School of Theology
www.krishk.com

Virginia Luckett – UK Churches Team Director, Tearfund
www.tearfund.org

Cathy Madavan – Author and speaker
www.cathymadavan.com

Medea Peabody – Co-director, Awaken Movement
www.awakenmovement.com

Rob Peabody – Co-founder and Global Director, Awaken
Movement
www.awakenmovement.com

Cris Rogers – Vicar and author
www.allhallowsbow.org.uk

Dot Tyler – Head of Youth and Young Adult Team, Tearfund
www.tearfund.org

Ruth Valerio – Churches and Theology Director, A Rocha
UK
www.ruthvalerio.net

We box Jesus in. We say, "This is how he works." But in answer to all the ways we aim to control, define and understand him, Jesus reminds us that he has immeasurably more to offer.

How often do we feel as if we are at the end of our energy? Not just physically and emotionally, but also spiritually? Some of us have been running this race for so long. We get so weary.

Jesus calls us all into a radical, empowered life that we couldn't ever achieve in our own strength. To a dehydrated church, Jesus announces: MORE is always on offer.

"A beautiful book by a remarkable leader exploring a magnificent theme. I commend it wholeheartedly to anyone thirsty for more from God."
– PETE GREIG, 24-7 Prayer

ISBN: 978-0-85721-637-3   £8.99/$13.99

www.lionhudson.com